National Health Insurance

Studies in Social Economics

TITLES PUBLISHED

STUDIES IN SOCIAL ECONOMICS

Karen Davis

National Health Insurance: Benefits, Costs, and Consequences

THE BROOKINGS INSTITUTION
Washington, D.C.

Copyright © 1975 by
THE BROOKINGS INSTITUTION
1775 Massachusetts Avenue, N.W., Washington, D.C. 20036

Library of Congress Cataloging in Publication Data:

Davis, Karen.
National health insurance.

(Studies in social economics)
Includes bibliographical references.
1. Insurance, Health—United States.   2. Medical
care—United States.   I. Title.   II. Series.   [DNLM:
1. Costs and cost analysis.   2. State medicine—
U.S. W275 AA1 D15n]
HD7102.U4D28   368.4′2′00973   75-5154
ISBN 0-8157-1760-1
ISBN 0-8157-1759-8 pbk.

9 8 7 6

Board of Trustees

Douglas Dillon
Chairman

Louis W. Cabot
Chairman,
Executive Committee

Vincent M. Barnett, Jr.
Lucy Wilson Benson
Edward W. Carter
George M. Elsey
John Fischer
Kermit Gordon
Huntington Harris
Roger W. Heyns
Luther G. Holbrook
William McC. Martin, Jr.
Robert S. McNamara
Arjay Miller
Barbara W. Newell
Herbert P. Patterson
J. Woodward Redmond
H. Chapman Rose
Warren M. Shapleigh
Gerard C. Smith
Phyllis A. Wallace
J. Harvie Wilkinson, Jr.

Honorary Trustees

Arthur Stanton Adams
Eugene R. Black
Robert D. Calkins
Colgate W. Darden, Jr.
Marion B. Folsom
John E. Lockwood
John Lee Pratt
Robert Brookings Smith
Sydney Stein, Jr.

THE BROOKINGS INSTITUTION is an independent organization devoted to nonpartisan research, education, and publication in economics, government, foreign policy, and the social sciences generally. Its principal purposes are to aid in the development of sound public policies and to promote public understanding of issues of national importance.

The Institution was founded on December 8, 1927, to merge the activities of the Institute for Government Research, founded in 1916, the Institute of Economics, founded in 1922, and the Robert Brookings Graduate School of Economics and Government, founded in 1924.

The Board of Trustees is responsible for the general administration of the Institution, while the immediate direction of the policies, program, and staff is vested in the President, assisted by an advisory committee of the officers and staff. The by-laws of the Institution state: "It is the function of the Trustees to make possible the conduct of scientific research, and publication, under the most favorable conditions, and to safeguard the independence of the research staff in the pursuit of their studies and in the publication of the results of such studies. It is not a part of their function to determine, control, or influence the conduct of particular investigations or the conclusions reached."

The President bears final responsibility for the decision to publish a manuscript as a Brookings book. In reaching his judgment on the competence, accuracy, and objectivity of each study, the President is advised by the director of the appropriate research program and weighs the views of a panel of expert outside readers who report to him in confidence on the quality of the work. Publication of a work signifies that it is deemed a competent treatment worthy of public consideration but does not imply endorsement of conclusions or recommendations.

The Institution maintains its position of neutrality on issues of public policy in order to safeguard the intellectual freedom of the staff. Hence interpretations or conclusions in Brookings publications should be understood to be solely those of the authors and should not be attributed to the Institution, to its trustees, officers, or other staff members, or to the organizations that support its research.

Foreword

For the last decade, health care has been a growing component in the federal budget. The Medicare and Medicaid programs, begun in 1966 to pay the health care bills of the elderly and the needy, are now major elements in federal and state expenditures. And new public and private organizations have been created to monitor the quality of health care, to plan the allocation of health resources, and to foster efficiency in the provision of health care.

Nonetheless, many deficiencies in the health care system remain, and it is widely maintained that the case for a unified, coordinated national health care policy is becoming steadily stronger. One major step that proponents of such a policy advocate is the enactment of legislation providing universal national health insurance coverage. In the last few years, more than twenty national health insurance bills have been introduced in Congress, diversely sponsored by organized medicine, the health insurance industry, labor unions, and businessmen. These proposals, however, differ markedly in approach and detail. With a bewildering array of choices before them, few citizens can sort out the best options, nor can they easily understand how they would be affected by various plans.

To clarify health care issues and choices, this study examines the distribution of benefits and costs associated with the seven major national health insurance plans embodied in proposed legislation. Without endorsing any one plan, the author outlines the features that best meet the objectives of national health insurance—ensuring access to medical care for all Americans, reducing the financial hardship of medical care bills, and improving efficiency in the provision of health care services.

The book is organized so that the first and last chapters can be read together as a brief summary of the major national health insurance issues. Chapter 2 shows why, in the author's view, sole reliance upon private initiative in the medical market will not work, and why she believes a greater role for government is desirable. Chapters 3 and 4 present evidence on the limitations of the current combination of private insurance and public health care programs, desiderata of a national health insurance plan, and criteria for choosing among alternative plans. Chapters 5, 6, and 7 describe the seven major proposals that have been introduced in Congress, apply to them the criteria developed in Chapter 4, estimate their costs and cost distribution among patients and taxpayers by income level, analyze how successful each is likely to be in meeting national health insurance goals, and assess how each would affect particular groups such as rural residents, racial minorities, and the poor.

Karen Davis is a senior fellow in the Brookings Economic Studies program. For reading and commenting on preliminary drafts, she is grateful to Joseph A. Pechman and Charles L. Schultze of the Brookings staff, Stuart Altman of the U.S. Department of Health, Education, and Welfare, Ray Marshall of the University of Texas, Bridger Mitchell of the Rand Corporation, Mark V. Pauly of the National Bureau of Economic Research and Northwestern University, Dorothy P. Rice of the Social Security Administration, and Alice M. Rivlin, formerly of Brookings and now of the Congressional Budget Office. The author was ably assisted by Roger A. Reynolds. The risk of factual error was minimized by the work of Evelyn P. Fisher. Charlotte Kaiser carried the major secretarial burden. Ellen A. Ash edited the manuscript; Florence Robinson prepared the index. The project was supported by grants from the Carnegie Corporation of New York and the Richard King Mellon Foundation for work on issues in federal budget policy and the Robert Wood Johnson Foundation for a study of health and poverty.

This is the twelfth volume in the Brookings Studies in Social Economics series. The series presents the results of research focused on selected problems in the fields of health, education, social security, and welfare.

The views expressed here are those of the author and should not be attributed to any of those whose assistance is acknowledged above, to the trustees, officers, or other staff members of the Brookings Institution, or to the Carnegie Corporation, the Richard King Mellon Foundation, or the Robert Wood Johnson Foundation.

KERMIT GORDON
President

May 1975
Washington, D.C.

Contents

ix

x

Figures

chapter one **A National Plan for Financing Health Care**

Unlike most major industrial countries, the United States has never had a comprehensive national plan for the provision of and payment for health care. While public programs at all levels of government affect the provision of health care in a multitude of ways, these programs lack a unifying policy designed to meet the health care needs of all Americans. It is not surprising, therefore, that some Americans fare well under the current mix of public programs and private initiatives while others are unassisted in their efforts to cope with the high cost of medical care.

Since the government has not developed a comprehensive public plan for meeting the costs of medical care, private institutions have assumed much of the responsibility for helping Americans to meet these costs. The private health insurance industry has grown from a $1 billion industry in 1950 to an expected $32 billion in 1975. This growth has been closely linked to the work place. About 80 percent of all private insurance is sold through employer groups. Thus, families that have an able-bodied, employed worker have been best served by this system—although workers often find that how good their coverage is depends largely on their employers. For those outside the work force, private insurance has been minimal.

In the mid-1960s, the federal government moved to assume responsibility for many of the people who were poorly served by the private system. Medicare and Medicaid were instituted to help the elderly and those on welfare, and more recently the permanently disabled, pay for medical care. In 1975, federal and state governments are expected to spend $25 billion under these programs. The government also provides indirect assistance to workers and their families through tax subsidies for the purchase of private health insurance and the payment of large medical bills. These tax subsidies result in an annual loss of $6 billion in federal tax revenues.

In spite of the phenomenal growth of private insurance and the large outlays by the government, many gaps remain. Over 6 million people below the poverty line are not covered by Medicaid, and few of the working poor have adequate private health insurance, if any. Less than 30 percent of the workers who lose their jobs and major source of income retain private health insurance coverage to protect them during this period when they are most vulnerable to the high cost of medical care. Even those covered by Medicare, Medicaid, or private health insurance plans often experience severe financial hardships because of restrictions on what is covered and how much will be paid.

Perhaps even more important, this patchwork approach to financing medical care has proved impotent in controlling high costs and has undoubtedly fostered much of the rapid inflation in medical care costs. The 1971–73 Economic Stabilization Program demonstrated that the rapid rise in medical care costs can be curbed—at least temporarily. A permanent solution, however, is likely only if medical care is financed under a single system that effectively uses the power of the purse to control costs.

Goals of National Health Insurance

While it is doubtful that any single plan can cope with *all* the ills of the health care system, it is increasingly recognized that genuine progress can be achieved only through reform of the method of paying for medical care that national health insurance addresses. A revamped payment system would make it possible to pursue programs to reorganize the delivery of health services, to upgrade the quality of care, and to promote the development of the right kinds of medical resources in the right places. National health insurance, however, is primarily concerned not with these important goals, but with those most easily achieved through financial mechanisms. Of these, three are of primary importance: (1) ensuring that all persons have access to medical care, (2) eliminating the financial hardship of medical bills, and (3) limiting the rise in health care costs.

Ensuring Access to Care

All Americans should have access to adequate high-quality medical care provided in a manner that respects their rights and personal dignity. At present, this goal is far from being reached.

While the Medicaid program, implemented in 1966, has helped many poor people obtain adequate medical care, almost 28 percent of the poor continue to be excluded from coverage. Private insurance has not filled this gap. Less than 40 percent of the poor in the labor force have even limited private health insurance, and only 11 percent have insurance for nonhospital services. Those poor who are covered by Medicaid have made dramatic gains in obtaining health care, and many now use medical services as extensively as people with higher incomes who have similar health problems, although the type and quality of care may differ. Those who have been excluded from Medicaid and private plans are lagging well behind the others in their use of medical services. The result for these unfortunate people is diminished health, reduced productivity, and needless suffering.

The United States can ill afford a work force that is restricted in productive capacity and a society whose quality of life is impaired because of sicknesses that could easily have been prevented or remedied at an early stage by more equitable application of the nation's medical technology. Meeting the needs of all those who cannot afford adequate medical care without some assistance must be a top priority of any national health insurance plan.

Eliminating Financial Hardship

With the rapid rise in medical care costs, the ability to afford adequate medical care is no longer a problem only for the poor. While public programs and private health insurance mitigate the problems many Americans face in meeting the high cost of medical care, they have failed to protect all people from the consequences of large medical bills. Over a million Americans are denied coverage because the insurance industry regards them as "uninsurable." People who work for small firms, who are self-employed, or who work in low-wage industries are frequently unable to purchase private insurance at group rates and must either go without insurance or pay exorbitant premiums for even limited coverage.

For families with large medical bills, private insurance is markedly inadequate. Only half of the population has any major medical coverage. For those who have major medical policies, limits on the expenditures that will be covered and requirements for sizable patient payments are the rule, not the exception. In a day when the average cost of health care for such conditions as terminal cancer exceeds $20,000, even those with some insurance can face bankrupting medical outlays.

Since the system of private insurance coverage has failed to protect all people from the consequences of large medical bills, the second major goal of national health insurance is to ensure that no family is forced to endure genuine financial hardship in obtaining needed medical care.

Limiting the Rise in Health Care Costs

National health insurance could also be one means of stemming the rising tide of medical care costs that is due in part to the present system, which covers some kinds of expenses but not others. The growth of private insurance and the implementation of Medicare and Medicaid have heightened awareness that the "wrong" kind of insurance—whether public or private—is partially to blame for the rise in medical costs. Historically, insurance polices have emphasized complete coverage for short hospital stays; therefore, patients may prefer to be hospitalized even when outpatient or nursing-home care would be cheaper. Hospitals have taken advantage of assured revenues from insurance plans to provide a wider range of sophisticated services—leading to ever rising costs. Complete coverage for short hospital stays under most insurance plans has also reduced incentives for patients and physicians to "police" the medical care market or to insist that services be efficiently produced and worth the resources devoted to them.

National health insurance could reverse many of these adverse effects. A comprehensive benefit plan with cost sharing,[1] for example, might help reduce the tendency of patients to choose hospital care over less expensive alternatives, curb runaway costs, and promote more efficient organization and delivery of medical services. Alternatively, financial controls and incentives for more efficient practices could be designed to promote these purposes, even without a centralized health insurance plan. However,

1. "Cost sharing" means any payments required of patients by deductible and coinsurance provisions.

tying the payment of medical services to cost controls undoubtedly provides the widest range of alternatives for combating high costs and promoting greater efficiency.

It should be recognized that, although a national health insurance plan
can be the instrument for restructuring the kinds of private insurance currently available and although it might discourage some types of excessive
insurance promoted in the private market, it can only achieve its goals of
ensuring access to medical care and limiting financial hardship by adding
to existing coverage in some cases. These increments in insurance coverage are likely to be inflationary, particularly if they are not offset by reductions in coverage for those expenses that are not a financial hardship.
If the plan covers all medical expenses above a certain limit, as it must to
provide good protection from financial hardship, excessive use of the most
costly medical technology may be encouraged. Clearly, regulatory mechanisms as well as automatic incentives for efficiency in the use of medical
resources are essential parts of a good national health insurance plan.

Supplementary Goals

A national health insurance plan meeting each of these three goals is
unlikely to be acceptable, however, unless it also (1) can be equitably
financed, (2) is easy to understand and administer, and (3) is acceptable
to providers of medical services and to the public.

An equitable method of financing is generally regarded as one that
does not fall more heavily on lower-income families than on higher-
income families. Financing for most national health insurance plans is
based on premiums, payroll tax revenues, and federal and state general
revenues. Financing by premiums is the most regressive method because
it requires a fixed amount from each family, regardless of income. The payroll tax is less regressive because it represents a fixed percentage of earnings, but since it does not affect other sources of income, such as interest,
dividends, rent, and capital gains, the tax typically represents a higher
share of total income for low-income families than for high-income
families.[2] Furthermore, if the payroll tax applies to only a limited portion
of earnings, as it does currently, it represents a declining share of income
for all families above the taxable base. General federal revenues, which
are drawn primarily from personal and corporate income taxes, are the

2. See Joseph A. Pechman and Benjamin A. Okner, *Who Bears the Tax Burden?* (Brookings Institution, 1974), pp. 58, 72, 78.

most progressive source of financing. State general revenues are derived largely from sales and property taxes and fall more heavily on low-income families.

Since the medical care system is inherently complex, it would be unrealistic to expect any national health insurance plan to meet all the special needs of the population in a simple fashion. Yet a plan cannot succeed if it is bewildering to those eligible for benefits. Some trade-offs between having a plan that is efficiently designed to achieve its major goals and having a plan that is understandable may be required. A plan that is so administratively complex that it causes long delays in reimbursement for services rendered and misunderstanding regarding what is covered and what is not can lead to disillusionment and disappointment with the system.

A national health insurance plan also must be acceptable to those responsible for its success—physicians, hospitals, and other providers of medical services—as well as patients. If the plan calls for a radical alteration of the relative income position of current providers or for sudden changes in current medical practices, considerable resistance to implementation can be expected. If patients feel that their views are not adequately represented and if there are no established grievance processes for voicing frustration about perceived inequities in the plan, the plan cannot function optimally. Thus, the greatest possible input from a wide range of views is essential in the planning, implementation, and ongoing administration of a national health insurance plan.

National Health Insurance: A Confusing Proliferation of Choices

While the goals of national health insurance are clear-cut and fairly widely agreed upon, the best approach to achieving these goals is much more open to question. More than twenty national health insurance bills were introduced in the Ninety-third Congress—ranging from bills that would provide federal tax subsidies to encourage more people to buy private health insurance to plans that would replace most private health insurance with a public plan. Some plans would cover all of the population, others would exclude certain segments. Some would replace the Medicare program for the elderly, some would modify it, and others would leave it alone. Some plans would be voluntary; others would automatically provide a specified health policy to everyone. Some would incorporate special plans for different groups; others call for a uniform plan for all persons. Some cover a wide range of medical services, including preventive services, family planning, maternity care, long-term care, and mental health services; others contain only a few of these benefits. A variety of methods for paying hospitals, physicians, and other health providers is to be found in the bills under consideration. Financing of the plans relies on a varied mix of revenues from state governments, employers, patients, and federal payroll taxes and general revenues.

While a broad consensus exists that a national plan should be adopted, the array of choices before the American people is indeed bewildering. Few people can sort out the best choice or even understand clearly how they would be affected by the various plans.

Even with a lawyer to explain the complexities of the bills, many important ramifications of alternative plans are simply not apparent. How much would each plan cost? In particular, how much could any given family expect to have to pay for the plan—either directly, through premium payments, taxes, or payments to hospitals and physicians, or indirectly, through reduced wages or higher prices? How would the plan change their present health insurance coverage for better or for worse? Would employers supplement a national plan if it were inadequate for their needs? Or, even harder to predict, if a community has few physicians or specialized medical facilities, could it expect that a plan would attract more medical resources to the area or would residents of the community wind up paying for medical care that someone else receives?

In spite of the complexity of national health insurance, it is essential to have widespread understanding of the implications of selecting any one approach. National health insurance, of whatever form, promises to have far-reaching effects and high costs. The health services industry is a $100 billion industry. Even without national health insurance, federal and state governments will be paying $25 billion for medical care services under Medicare and Medicaid in 1975. The most modest proposals would raise this to about $35 billion; one would increase it to almost $100 billion. Although some of the plans would not significantly increase government expenditures, they could radically alter the composition of private payments—among employers and workers and among families at various income levels.

This study is an attempt to focus greater attention on the costs, benefits, and consequences of national health insurance and to foster greater understanding of the implications of alternative approaches.

chapter two **Health Care, the Private Market,**
and Public Policy

While health care services in the United States are
for the most part privately provided, in recent years government has
played an increasingly important role. Federal, state, and local governments have major commitments to finance medical care for the poor, disabled, and elderly and now pay almost 40 percent of all the nation's
health care bills.[1] The federal government not only helps pay for medical
services but sponsors medical research, provides funds for training health
professionals, and underwrites the development of medical facilities. In
1976, it is expected that 11 percent of the federal budget will go to health
care and related activities.[2]

At the same time the government is pouring billions of dollars into the
health care sector of the economy, it is demonstrating increasing concern
and control over the services purchased either directly or indirectly with
these funds. In recent years, legislation has expanded government in-
volvement in monitoring the kind and quality of medical care provided,
in controlling health care costs, and in planning and regulating health
care facilities. State and local governments have long assumed responsibility for licensing health care providers, regulating the provision of insurance for health services, and providing certain essential medical services to those unable to pay.

1. Barbara S. Cooper, Nancy L. Worthington, and Paula A. Piro, "National
Health Expenditures, 1929–73," *Social Security Bulletin,* vol. 37 (February 1974),
p. 3.
2. *Special Analyses, Budget of the United States Government, Fiscal Year
1976,* p. 169. For an analysis of major trends in the federal budget see Barry M.
Blechman, Edward M. Gramlich, and Robert W. Hartman, *Setting National Priorities: The 1975 Budget* (Brookings Institution, 1974).

8

Rationale for Government Action

The major role played by government in the health care sector, and proposed extensions of this role, are based on the desire to correct three deficiencies inherent in the private provision of health care services. First, without assistance many lower-income people will not buy the medical care required to help them lead longer, more productive, and enjoyable lives. Second, prevailing types of health insurance do not encourage an efficient use of medical resources. Third, limited information and a lack of competition in the medical care market contribute to high medical costs.

Medical Care and the Poor

While medical care is only one factor contributing to health, it is often a matter of life and death. Many people die or become permanently disabled from afflictions that today's medical technology can prevent.[3] Special programs to improve prenatal medical care have markedly reduced infant mortality,[4] but, for many poor people, financial barriers to medical care still result in needless death. Children become blinded or suffer a permanent hearing loss from conditions that simple medical examinations could have detected and that adequate care could have reversed.[5] Many major causes of death, such as heart disease and, to a lesser extent, cancer, cannot be prevented or quickly ameliorated by modern medicine, but the

3. Leon Gordis, for example, has documented the dramatic decline in the incidence of rheumatic fever brought about by comprehensive health care centers in Baltimore. ("Effectiveness of Comprehensive-Care Programs in Preventing Rheumatic Fever," *New England Journal of Medicine,* vol. 289 [Aug. 16, 1973], pp. 331–35.) See also Victor R. Fuchs, "The Contribution of Health Services to the American Economy," in Victor R. Fuchs (ed.), *Essays in the Economics of Health and Medical Care* (Columbia University Press for the National Bureau of Economic Research, 1972), for a discussion of the link between medical care and health.

4. *National Health Insurance Resource Book,* prepared by the Staff of the House Committee on Ways and Means (1974), pp. 499–501.

5. For a discussion of the permanent disabling effects of inadequate nutrition and medical care in early childhood, see Raymond Wheeler, "Health and Human Resources," *New South,* vol. 26 (Fall 1971), pp. 2–16. Dr. Wheeler and a team of physicians examining poor children for the Citizens Board of Inquiry into Hunger in the United States uncovered diseases, such as rickets, believed to have been eradicated in the United States.

poor, particularly in rural areas and among minority groups, have high rates of mortality from curable diseases of early infancy, infectious diseases, and respiratory ailments.[6] The link between deaths from these causes and limited contact with the medical system is clear. Almost 3 million children under the age of fourteen have never been vaccinated against the dread diseases of diphtheria, tetanus, and whooping cough; 40 percent of all children between the ages of one and four are not protected against polio; and 40 percent of children under the age of thirteen have not received rubella vaccine.[7] Low immunization rates are particularly characteristic of the children of minorities and of children in central cities and rural areas. But the effects of failing to spread the benefits of medical technology are not restricted to children. Only 20 to 25 percent of the elderly with known debilitating conditions received influenza vaccine during 1972. Chronic conditions, such as diabetes and hypertension, go untreated or are only sporadically managed among those unable to afford adequate care. Migrant workers can look forward to a low life expectancy because of inadequate medical care, exposure to harmful health conditions, and all the consequences of poverty.

Many of these health problems cannot be totally eradicated by reducing the financial barrier to medical care; adequate incomes for all, sound nutrition, better sanitation, improved water supplies, and better housing will be required for that. However, making medical care more accessible to those with limited means is an important first step.

On the other hand, for some poor people, medical care serves primarily to reduce pain, alleviate symptoms, and relieve anxiety. These benefits of medical care are less likely to lead to marked improvements in worker productivity. Yet, they are no less worthwhile, and society should be no more willing to deny these benefits of medical care to the poor than to deny them adequate housing simply because housing might not extend their lives or increase gross national product.

Without financial assistance, the poor cannot obtain the kind and amount of medical care they require or afford health insurance that will spread the cost of care among those with more severe health problems

6. Milton I. Roemer, "Health Needs and Services of the Rural Poor," in *Rural Poverty in the United States,* a Report by the President's National Advisory Committee on Rural Poverty (U.S. Government Printing Office, 1968).

7. U.S. Department of Health, Education, and Welfare, Center for Disease Control, *United States Immunization Survey: 1972,* DHEW (HSM) 73-8221 (1973); and *New York Times,* editorial, October 8, 1974.

and those with somewhat lower needs for medical care. Even with substantial increases in income through improved income maintenance programs, the poor are still apt to view medical care as a luxury to be in-
dulged in only after the pressing demands for adequate shelter, clothing,
and food have been met. Although they may have some form of medical
insurance, many families with modest earnings who are not assisted by
an income maintenance program also may encounter difficulty in purchasing costly medical care.

Increasingly, therefore, it has become accepted that for a given health
problem the poor should have as much access to medical care as those
who can afford to pay. Furthermore, those who do not have the financial
resources to purchase medical care should not be subjected to the indig-
nities, inconvenience, long delays, and inferior quality that have long
characterized charity medical care.

Private Health Insurance and the Optimal Use of Medical Services

Most national health insurance proposals are concerned not just with
the poor or with those whose health insurance payments take a large fraction of their earnings, but with higher-income people—many of whom
are currently covered by private health insurance plans. Some proposals
would require Americans to give up their current insurance for a different
type of plan, or would offer inducements to do so. Why should national
health insurance attempt to change the kind of coverage currently held by
many?

The attempt to restructure insurance coverage is based on evidence
that present insurance provides excessive coverage for short hospital
stays, insufficient coverage for large medical expenses, and insufficient
coverage for lower-cost alternatives to hospitalization. Furthermore, it is
unavailable to many Americans. To understand the forces behind this
situation requires an exploration of the influence of insurance on the use
and cost of medical services; institutional factors that markedly affect the
purchase of insurance—particularly tax subsidies for insurance and
coverage through employer groups; the historical relationship between
the insurance industry and major providers of medical services; and
finally, the divergence between the interests of insurance companies and
those of consumers caused by special characteristics of the insurance
market.

INSURANCE AND THE COST OF MEDICAL CARE. The purchase of

health insurance has both advantages and disadvantages. The basic purpose of insurance is to provide families with assurance that in the event of serious illness they will not be doubly unfortunate by also incurring very large medical expenses. The peace of mind this reduction in risk offers is sufficient to induce many families to purchase insurance even if the premium cost *on average* is greater than the cost of paying for medical services directly. In general, health insurance is likely to be more costly than paying for medical services directly for at least two reasons.

First, insurance companies must be compensated for their costs of doing business, including advertising and sales costs, cost of handling claims, administrative costs, and return to capital investment, as well as claims expenses. The average costs of most group health insurance plans are 10 to 11 percent higher than the payments the insurance company makes to physicians, hospitals, and other medical care providers on behalf of patients. Out of every dollar of health insurance sold directly to individuals rather than through group plans, at least 47 cents go for nonmedical care expenses.

Second, the total amount spent for medical care is likely to be greater with insurance than it would be if the family purchased medical care directly. Insurance has the effect of making medical care less costly to families; a family thus has an incentive both to purchase more medical care than it would have without insurance and to choose more costly forms of medical care.[8] If all families covered by the insurance plan behave this way, the premium cost will go up for everyone. However, once insured, it is to each family's advantage to behave in this manner since the premium will not be directly affected by the choices the family makes.

A growing number of studies have documented that families do respond in just this way to insurance coverage. Insured families have more hospitalizations, longer hospital stays, more visits to the physician, and more extensive use of ancillary services such as laboratory tests and X-ray examinations.[9] Furthermore, as insurance policies cover a larger

8. This characteristic of health care insurance was noted by Mark V. Pauly, "The Economics of Moral Hazard: Comment," *American Economic Review*, vol. 58 (June 1968), pp. 531–37.

9. For summaries of some of the relevant findings, see Martin S. Feldstein, "Econometric Studies of Health Economics," Discussion Paper 291 (Harvard University, Harvard Institute of Economic Research, 1973; processed); Paul B. Ginsburg and Larry M. Manheim, "Insurance, Copayment, and Health Services Utiliza-

and larger share of the total medical bill, incentives to make even more use of medical services, and particularly more expensive types of service, are compounded.

Experts differ about whether this increased use of medical services is good or bad for patients. There are indications that some patients may be receiving "too much" care; for example, they may receive surgery for conditions that do not require resort to this extreme method.[10] The major point, however, is that families with insurance receive medical services they do not value sufficiently to obtain if required to pay for the services directly. Yet, the families do pay ultimately in the form of higher insurance premiums.

The fact that insurance raises the cost of a family's medical care would be of little concern to policymakers if families decided to buy insurance only after carefully weighing all of the advantages and disadvantages of doing so. The extent of insurance coverage purchased privately would then reflect consideration of the benefits of a reduced risk of incurring large medical expenditures in relation to the higher cost of purchasing medical care through health insurance. There is ample reason to believe, however, that a number of factors intervene to prevent families from taking into account all of the costs of health insurance and from making their decision on the basis of benefits and costs.

One source of policy concern is that the consequences of health insurance provisions affect all members of society, not just those choosing to purchase insurance. Instead, the growth of private health insurance (and public programs that pay for medical care) has led to a change in the cost, quality, and types of medical services that are available to all people, insured or not. Insurance has made it possible for physicians to charge higher fees for the same services.[11] Medicare and Medicaid have brought hospital-based physicians, such as anesthesiologists, radiologists, and

---

tion: A Critical Review," *Journal of Economics and Business,* vol. 25 (Winter 1973), pp. 142–53; and Joseph P. Newhouse and Charles E. Phelps, *On Having Your Cake and Eating It Too: Economic Problems in Estimating the Demand for Health Services,* R-1149-NC (Rand Corporation, 1974).

10. John P. Bunker, "Surgical Manpower: A Comparison of Operations and Surgeons in the United States and in England and Wales," *New England Journal of Medicine,* vol. 282 (January 5, 1970), pp. 135–44.

11. See Victor R. Fuchs and Marcia J. Kramer, *Determinants of Expenditures for Physicians' Services in the United States, 1948–68,* DHEW Publication (HSM) 73-3013 (1972); and Martin S. Feldstein, "The Rising Price of Physicians' Services," *Review of Economics and Statistics,* vol. 52 (May 1970), pp. 121–33.

pathologists, added opportunity to increase their incomes. Even nurses and other hospital workers who had traditionally been paid low wages benefited from the increased revenues available to hospitals.[12] These higher costs are reflected in the bills of all patients.

Insurance has also altered the quality and range of medical services available to patients. Hospitals, particularly, have responded to the growth of insurance coverage—both public and private—by providing a more expensive style of hospital care.[13] About half of the increase in hospital costs over the 1951–70 period reflected additional inputs to provide a day of hospital care.[14] This change in the nature of hospital care has affected all patients, regardless of their individual insurance choices.

Furthermore, the effect of insurance on the cost of medical care causes more individuals to purchase insurance as protection against rising prices and induces those with partial insurance to obtain more complete coverage. As Feldstein described it, "People spend more on health because they are insured and buy more insurance because of the high cost of health care."[15] The desire to curb this spiral underlies the promulgation of national health insurance plans that retain considerable direct consumer participation in paying the cost of medical care. Insurance coverage for hospital services has become so extensive and the resultant costs of hospital services so high that even a one-third reduction in the extent of hospital insurance, it is estimated, would result in a net gain of several billion dollars a year.[16]

TAX SUBSIDIES AND THE PURCHASE OF INSURANCE. Taxpayers as a group also help pay for the health insurance of insured families through various tax subsidies.[17] These tax subsidies are so extensive that many

12. See Karen Davis, "Rising Hospital Costs: Possible Causes and Cures," *Bulletin of the New York Academy of Medicine*, vol. 48 (December 1972), pp. 1354–71 (Brookings Reprint 262); and Martin S. Feldstein, *The Rising Cost of Hospital Care* (Information Resources Press, 1971), chap. 5.

13. Martin S. Feldstein, "Hospital Cost Inflation: A Study of Nonprofit Price Dynamics," *American Economic Review*, vol. 61 (December 1971), pp. 853–72.

14. Saul Waldman, "The Effect of Changing Technology on Hospital Costs," *Research and Statistics Note*, No. 4-1972 (Social Security Administration, Office of Research and Statistics, 1972), p. 2.

15. Martin S. Feldstein, "The Welfare Loss of Excess Health Insurance," *Journal of Political Economy*, vol. 81 (March–April 1973), p. 252.

16. Ibid., p. 251.

17. For an analysis of who benefits from tax subsidies for health care, see Karen Davis, "Financing Medical Care Services: The Federal Role," in *Medical Policies and Costs*, Hearings before the Subcommittee on Consumer Economics of the Joint Economic Committee, 93 Cong. 1 sess. (1973), pp. 69–76 (Brook-

families find it cheaper to purchase medical care indirectly through health insurance than to pay for the services as they are received.

These subsidies are provided in two ways. First, under the personal income tax, one-half of the cost of health insurance premiums up to $150, plus all medical expenses (including the remaining premiums) that exceed 3 percent of income, may be deducted on each tax return. Second, the fact that employers' contributions to health insurance for employees are not taxable as income results in a loss of revenue from both the personal income and payroll taxes to the government. The federal government thus subsidizes the purchase of health insurance both by individuals and by employers on their employees' behalf.[18]

Estimates indicate that the federal government lost $5.6 billion in tax revenues in 1974 as a result of these provisions.[19] Approximately $3 billion is attributable to the exclusion of employers' contributions to health insurance plans from taxable income, while the remaining $2.6 billion represents lost revenue from personal income tax deductions. The size of this tax subsidy is comparable to the total federal contribution to Medicaid, which finances medical care for the poor, and represents about 17 per-

---

ings Reprint 278); Martin S. Feldstein and Elizabeth Allison, "Tax Subsidies of Private Health Insurance: Distribution, Revenue Loss and Effects," Discussion Paper 237 (Harvard University, Harvard Institute of Economic Research, 1972); and Bridger M. Mitchell and Ronald J. Vogel, *Health and Taxes: An Assessment of the Medical Deduction,* R-1222-OEO (Rand Corporation, 1973).

18. Estimates of the tax subsidy for employer contributions typically are made on the assumption that the employer's contribution toward a health insurance plan is a substitute for higher wages. The federal government therefore loses tax revenues it would have derived from the higher wages. If the cost of the employer's contribution is passed on to consumers in higher prices with no change in wages or profits, then federal tax revenue is unchanged, but the cost of governmental services is increased. Thus, the real value of federal tax revenues is reduced. For an analysis of who bears payroll taxes and similar costs of labor, see John A. Brittain, *The Payroll Tax for Social Security* (Brookings Institution, 1972).

19. Estimate from Davis, "Financing Medical Care Services," p. 74; Mitchell and Vogel estimated a total tax subsidy of $3.8 billion in 1970, split equally between the employer contribution subsidy and the personal income tax deduction. (*Health and Taxes,* p. 1.) Feldstein and Allison estimated that federal income and social security tax revenues would have been $1.63 billion higher in 1969 if employer contributions to health insurance had been considered taxable income. ("Tax Subsidies of Private Health Insurance," p. 2.) In a more recent study, Mitchell and Phelps estimated this revenue loss to be $2.542 billion in 1970. (Bridger M. Mitchell and Charles E. Phelps, "Employer-Paid Group Health Insurance and the Costs of Mandated National Coverage" [Rand Corporation, 1974; processed], p. 18.)

Table 2-1. Loading Rates[a] on Group Health Insurance Policies before and after Tax Subsidies, by Annual Family Income Class, 1970

Income class (dollars)	Loading rate on group insurance premiums (percent)	Tax subsidy as a percent of premiums[b]	Net loading rate (percent)[b]
All classes	10.8	16.7	−5.9
Under 3,000	14.7	8.6	6.0
3,000–5,000	10.6	14.7	−4.1
5,000–7,000	10.2	15.4	−5.3
7,000–10,000	9.6	16.6	−6.9
10,000–15,000	11.3	15.2	−4.0
15,000–20,000	11.5	17.7	−6.2
20,000–50,000	11.5	23.8	−12.3
50,000–100,000[c]	10.0	36.9	−26.9

Source: Bridger M. Mitchell and Charles E. Phelps, "Employer-Paid Group Health Insurance and the Costs of Mandated National Coverage" (Rand Corporation, 1974; processed), table 7, p. 17. Calculations were made from data before rounding.

a. Loading rate can best be explained by the following example. If the premium is $500 and the insurance company pays out $450 to cover medical bills, the remainder (called "the cost of insurance") is $50, which goes to profits, administrative expenses, overhead, etc. The cost of the insurance divided by the premium equals the loading rate—50/500 = 10 percent.

b. Calculated on the basis of the 1973 tax law, which through the low-income allowance excludes low-income families and individuals from tax obligations.

c. One observation.

cent of total health insurance premium payments. It is not surprising, therefore, that the subsidy has had a major impact on the extent of private insurance coverage.

In a recent study, Mitchell and Phelps compared the magnitude of the tax subsidy with the cost of insurance (defined as the difference between premium payments and benefit expenses, or the loading factor).[20] As shown in Table 2-1, they found that with the exception of the lowest-income families (who typically work for small firms with high insurance loading rates and whose marginal tax rates and amount of tax subsidies are low) the extent of the tax subsidy is greater than the cost of insurance. The cost of group insurance averaged 11 percent of benefits, but the federal government "paid" 17 percent of the premium through tax subsidies. Thus, the average cost of medical care for an insured family was 6 percent less than it would have been if the family had purchased the same amount of medical care directly. For families with incomes above $20,000, the cost savings of indirect payment of medical expenses was much greater.

Given the strong incentives to purchase insurance offered by present

20. Mitchell and Phelps, "Employer-Paid Group Health Insurance," pp. 11–18.

tax provisions, it is obvious why many people prefer comprehensive insurance—even if the insurance results in increased use of medical services, inflated charges for health care, and higher insurance premiums. Excessive insurance coverage for some kinds of services, therefore, can be directly traced to current tax policy.

If tax subsidies were the only major cause of excessive insurance coverage, there would be little reason to correct the imbalance through national health insurance. Instead, elimination of the tax subsidy provisions would be a logical course. Unfortunately, a number of other forces give rise to extensive hospital insurance coverage, limited coverage for alternatives to hospitalization, and the exclusion of some high-risk people from any insurance plan.

EMPLOYER GROUP INSURANCE AND COLLECTIVE BARGAINING. In most studies of the economics of insurance, it is assumed that each individual or family unit decides what insurance to purchase, if any.[21] Individually purchased insurance, however, represents only a small fraction of insurance sold. Group health insurance accounts for about 80 percent of all health insurance premium payments.[22]

For employer group insurance to reflect the preferences of every employee, a number of extremely stringent conditions would be required. Workers would have to have a wide range of employment choices so that the decision to select any one job could be made on the basis of an optimal package of wages, health insurance, and other benefits. Otherwise, firms would need to be large enough to offer different insurance policies to groups of workers with different sets of preferences.

But even if employers desired and were able to offer insurance that represented the wishes of all employees, the process of collective bargain-

---

21. Kenneth J. Arrow, "Uncertainty and the Welfare Economics of Medical Care," *American Economic Review*, vol. 53 (December 1963), pp. 941–73; Bernard S. Friedman, "A Study of Uncertainty and Health Insurance" (Ph.D. dissertation, Massachusetts Institute of Technology, 1971); Charles E. Phelps, *Demand for Health Insurance: A Theoretical and Empirical Investigation*, R-1054-OEO (Rand Corporation, 1973); and Richard Zeckhauser, "Medical Insurance: A Case Study of the Tradeoff between Risk Spreading and Appropriate Incentives," *Journal of Economic Theory*, vol. 2 (March 1970), pp. 10–26.

22. Marjorie S. Mueller, "Private Health Insurance in 1970: Population Coverage, Enrollment, and Financial Experience," *Social Security Bulletin*, vol. 35 (February 1972), p. 5. For a description of the characteristics of workers covered by group health insurance plans, see Walter W. Kolodrubetz, "Group Health Insurance Coverage of Full-Time Employees, 1972," *Social Security Bulletin*, vol. 37 (April 1974), pp. 17–35.

ing could result in a quite different kind of insurance. Unions are primarily concerned with union members, not with employees as a group. Goldstein and Pauly have pointed out that, while group insurance may be open to all employees, nonunion members usually are women or low-income and young male workers who are likely to have lower demands for insurance than union members.[23] Therefore, unions may well press for more comprehensive insurance than many employees desire. Vickrey argues that unions may be more concerned with senior members than with all union members, and senior members are likely to prefer more extensive insurance.[24] Union members may also make compromises among themselves; younger members may concede better pension benefits in exchange for concessions from older members for maternity benefits or other health benefits of primary concern to the young.

The predominance of group insurance and the importance of collective bargaining in the determination of health insurance may also explain why an executive of the health insurance industry has estimated that "about one million individuals . . . are presently uninsurable."[25] If bad risks are included in a group, the cost of coverage will be higher for other members. Good risks (or those anticipating low medical expenditures) may drop out, or, if they constitute a majority, they may pressure employers or unions to use exclusionary devices, such as medical examinations or strict job requirements, to deny coverage to those with high expected medical expenditures. Even if bad risks are admitted to a plan, costs may be held down by excluding preexisting conditions from coverage or by setting ceilings on the medical expenses that will be covered. The private health insurance industry has declined to sell insurance against the possibility of becoming a poor risk, but instead insists on adjusting premiums upward or refusing coverage to anyone who encounters severe medical problems.

To the extent that employers pay all or part of the premium for group insurance, employees may assume that employer payments for health insurance do not result in a corresponding decrease in money income.

23. See Gerald S. Goldstein and Mark V. Pauly, "Group Health Insurance as a Local Public Good," in Richard N. Rosett (ed.), *The Role of Health Insurance in the Health Services Sector,* A Conference of the Universities–National Bureau Committee for Economic Research (National Bureau of Economic Research, 1975).

24. William Vickrey, "Comments" on Goldstein-Pauly paper, in ibid.

25. George L. Hogeman, president, Paul Revere Life Insurance Company, testimony in *National Health Insurance—Implications,* Hearings before the Subcommittee on Public Health and Environment of the House Committee on Interstate and Foreign Commerce, 93 Cong. 1 sess., 2 sess. (1974), p. 327.

This may reinforce other strong incentives for comprehensive insurance. Furthermore, unions and employers may desire that benefits be clearly visible to employees so that small routine medical expenses are covered while catastrophic expenses of very low probability are not.[26]

BLUE CROSS AND THE HOSPITAL INDUSTRY. Private health insurance has focused primarily on medical services rendered within a hospital. Coverage of physician services outside the hospital has been more limited, while nonhospital prescription drugs and dental care are typically excluded from basic insurance coverage. Private-duty nursing care, even if provided in a hospital, is rarely covered, except under major medical plans with sizable deductibles. Failure to cover these services may reflect both the lower share of these medical costs in family budgets and the greater degree of choice patients have in the purchase of these services. Many of these services, however, can be financial burdens to patients—such as prescription drugs for chronically ill patients—and are no more or less "patient initiated" than hospital stays.

Health insurance policies also frequently exclude alternatives to hospitalization—such as outpatient hospital care, nursing-home care, or care in a surgicenter—even though costs may be lower. Again, part of the explanation may lie in a fear that if these less costly substitutes for inpatient care were included in more extensive insurance coverage the demand for them would increase, driving up costs and reducing the attractiveness of the policy to potential buyers.

However, the historical development of hospital insurance and its close ties to the hospital industry suggest that much of the current insurance is designed to serve medical care providers rather than to protect consumers. Blue Cross, which sells 40 percent of hospital insurance, had its start during the Depression of the 1930s. As Law has noted:

Hospitals were hard hit by the Depression. In one year, from 1929 to 1930, the average hospital receipts per patient fell from $236.12 to $59.26. Average per cent of occupancy fell from 71.28 per cent to 64.12 per cent. Average deficits as a percentage of disbursements rose from 15.2 per cent to 20. 6 per cent. The hospitals had an immediate interest in developing a stable source of payment for services and also had the technical and financial resources to create such a program. Of 39 Blue Cross plans established in the early 1930s, 22 obtained all of their initial funds from hospitals, and five were partially financed by hospitals.[27]

26. See Feldstein, "The Welfare Loss of Excess Health Insurance," pp. 253–55.

27. Sylvia A. Law, *Blue Cross: What Went Wrong?* (Yale University Press, 1974), pp. 6–7.

Hospital insurance was started, therefore, primarily to provide hospitals with an assured source of revenue. Close ties between Blue Cross and the hospital industry have continued. Until 1972, the Blue Cross name and insignia were owned by the American Hospital Association (AHA). Interlocking directorships between the Blue Cross Association (the national trade association) and AHA were also continued until that time. A Blue Cross plan must be a nonprofit community service organization, with a governing board comprised of representatives of the providers of the service and of the public. In 1970, 56 percent of Blue Cross local board members were medical providers, with 42 percent of these representing hospitals and 14 percent representing the medical profession. In most cases, public board representatives are selected by the incumbent board, but in some cases, they are selected by hospital representatives. In 1971, only eight Blue Cross plans had elected public members. The fact that only 18 out of 824 public members of local plan boards were women suggests that the selection process is less than representative of all consumers.[28]

While Blue Cross might be expected to push the sale of policies that favor hospitalization rather than lower-cost alternatives, the same would not hold for commercial competitors. Commercial insurance companies, however, have been at a disadvantage because of the preferential treatment afforded Blue Cross. Blue Cross is exempt from federal taxes (and in most states from state taxes), and the hospitals in most plans require it to pay only on the basis of costs, while other companies are required to pay whatever a hospital charges.

OTHER CHARACTERISTICS OF THE INSURANCE MARKET. While tax provisions, group insurance, and the predominance of Blue Cross are the major forces affecting the extent of private insurance, certain difficulties in providing insurance also affect coverage. Perhaps the most important of these is the inability of those offering insurance to obtain accurate information about the health of those seeking it. Consumers are far more likely to understand the extent and severity of their incipient health problems than an insuring agent. Even compulsory medical examinations may not uncover important problems if the patient deliberately hides or does not volunteer symptoms or medical history information. Insurance companies have tried to reduce this inherent disadvantage by pooling their computer data banks on patient medical histories. But in spite of such

28. Ibid., pp. 18–30.

tactics, the companies may well decline to offer coverage of large medical expenses for fear they will attract, and be unable to screen, abnormally high medical risks.

Full coverage of medical services also removes any automatic constraints on medical care prices. Thus, if an insurance company guarantees those who are covered that it will pick up all medical expenses regardless of the size of the bill, providers, such as specialist physicians, may demand exorbitant fees for their services. Insurance companies have preferred to sell policies that reimburse physicians on the basis of preestablished fee schedules, making the patient responsible for any excess.

In sum, there is little assurance that the purchase of insurance reflects a careful appraisal of the advantages and disadvantages of coverage. Instead, it is clear that the market offers many incentives to families to buy more comprehensive insurance than they would otherwise desire. Thus, the cost of medical care is driven up, and many families may be worse off than they would have been if fewer of them had been covered by extensive insurance plans.

It is clear, however, that the private market provides too little rather than too much insurance for some families. Some high-risk people are excluded from coverage. In addition, policies that would place limits on patients' financial liability have not been widely offered; instead, limits are placed on maximum amounts that will be paid by the plan. Coverage of ambulatory care and lower-cost alternatives to hospitalization has not been promoted. Some workers must take jobs in firms that provide only the most limited coverage—which proves to be completely inadequate in a medical crisis.

Medical Care Market

Although the growth of insurance is widely recognized as a major cause of rapidly rising medical costs and the growing proportion of the gross national product devoted to health care, these changes could not have come about if the provision of medical services took place in a competitive market. But the medical care market has many characteristics not found in the provision of most goods and services.

LIMITED INFORMATION. The nature of health care is such that the consumer knows very little about the medical services he or she is buying—possibly less than about any other service purchased. Some choices about medical care are made solely by patients. But a very large part of the decisionmaking is done by physicians—diagnosis, treatment, drugs and tests, hospitalization, frequency of return visits are all substantially under the physician's control. Those who provide medical care can, to a large extent, create the demand for their own services. While the consumer can still participate in policing the market, that participation is much more limited in the field of health care than in almost any other area of private economic activity.

A patient's preferences regarding the kind and cost-mix of services may be taken into account by his or her physician, particularly by one who considers it a responsibility to act as the patient's agent, making choices that the patient would make if perfectly informed.[29] It is not unreasonable, however, to suspect that a physician's decisions will reflect not only a strong sense of professional ethics but pressures from peers and considerable self-interest as well. Financial self-interest is curbed in several ways. The practice of obtaining several opinions on the necessity of surgery is one example. Malpractice suits are another. But some studies have suggested that physicians often do recommend excessive amounts of medical care. The United States, for example, has twice as many surgeons per capita as England and twice as many surgeries per capita,[30] and it has been shown that there is a direct relationship between increases in the number of hospital admissions and increases in the supply of physicians, particularly specialists.[31] There is also considerable evidence that an increased demand for physicians follows an increased supply.[32] Therefore, solutions to rising medical costs—such as increasing the supply of physicians—that rely on simple shifts in the balance between supply and demand may not work and could actually lead to higher costs without some basic changes in incentives.

MONOPOLISTIC ELEMENTS. Abuses stemming from the limited information available to patients are aggravated by monopolistic elements in the medical care market. Numerous studies have detailed evidence of

29. See Feldstein, "Econometric Studies of Health Economics."

30. Bunker, "Surgical Manpower," p. 136.

31. Feldstein, "Hospital Cost Inflation," and Karen Davis and Louise B. Russell, "The Substitution of Hospital Outpatient Care for Inpatient Care," *Review of Economics and Statistics,* vol. 54 (May 1972), pp. 109–20.

32. Feldstein, "Rising Price of Physicians' Services"; Fuchs and Kramer, *Determinants of Expenditures for Physicians' Services;* and Donald E. Yett and Frank A. Sloan, "Analysis of Migration Patterns of Recent Medical School Graduates" (paper presented at the Health Services Research Conference on Factors in Health Manpower Performance and the Delivery of Health Care, Chicago, Dec. 9, 1971; processed).

imperfect competition, particularly in the market for physicians.[33] Licensing provisions, restricted entry to medical school, and sanctions against advertising and overt price competition are just a few of the features of this market that deter competition.

Nonetheless, in recent years, the number of physicians has increased substantially. Federal funds that provide support to medical schools on a student capitation basis have made it possible to expand enrollments somewhat. In addition, students who have been unable to find openings in U.S. medical schools have gone abroad and are now returning to practice in ever-increasing numbers. This growth in numbers, however, is unlikely to noticeably improve competitive conditions if the physician's control of the marketplace remains unchanged.

Licensing provisions that require virtually all types of medical care to be performed only by physicians or under their supervision limit the expansion of independent paramedical personnel. Continued restrictions on information available to patients about the cost of alternative treatment methods and about the quality of and necessity for treatment can continue to enhance the share of financial resources going to physicians. Some states have also blocked the growth of prepaid group plans that place physicians on salaries and eliminate their incentive to provide expensive services.

Hospital care, though provided primarily by nonprofit organizations, also contains numerous noncompetitive conditions. Oligopolistic pricing agreements among hospitals are commonplace, and there is little fear of antitrust action. Patients are restricted in their choice of hospitals to those with which their physicians are affiliated. Limited information about costs and the qualty of care at alternative hospitals makes rational choice difficult even when several alternatives are available.

Major Options for Federal Action

A wide range of choices confronts the policymakers who must decide how to correct or ameliorate the shortcomings of the private market. One

33. See, for example, Arrow, "Uncertainty and the Welfare Economics of Medical Care"; Milton Friedman and Simon Kuznets, *Income from Independent Professional Practice* (National Bureau of Economic Research, 1945), pp. 237–60; Reuben A. Kessel, "Price Discrimination in Medicine," *Journal of Law and Economics,* vol. 1 (October 1958), pp. 20–53; and Joseph P. Newhouse, "A Model of Physician Pricing," *Southern Economic Journal,* vol. 37 (October 1970), pp. 174–83.

possible decision is that the workings of a private market are beyond remedy and that public provision of medical care services is in order. At the other extreme, it might be decided that the shortcomings of the private market are largely the result of current government intervention, which should be reduced. For example, tax subsidies that promote the sale of private insurance could be eliminated, regulations that restrict the entry of new medical care providers into the market could be removed, and curbs on payments to physicians and hospitals under public medical care programs could be discontinued. Such actions, however, are unlikely to help the poor gain access to medical care or to eliminate financial hardship for those with inadequate insurance coverage. But any of these actions that hold the promise of reducing the costs of medical care should be explored—particularly the reform of tax subsidies.

A somewhat less extreme but still basically conservative viewpoint is that, although the private market is admittedly inefficient, any attempt by government to rectify this situation would only lead to further inefficiency. Additional government expenditures, for example, would require higher taxes, which could have adverse effects on work incentives. More effective controls on medical care prices might destroy some important functions of prices in attracting more practitioners to appropriate areas. Income maintenance for the poor might enable most poor people to receive adequate medical care, eliminating the necessity for direct intervention in the medical care market. While these possible government actions and their outcomes should be recognized, experience under current programs does not permit the sanguine view that the private market will perform adequately if left alone. A positive expanded role for government is clearly called for.

This expanded role could take many forms. Even if for historical or other reasons it were decided to continue the private provision of medical care, the market could be altered either indirectly by providing consumers with appropriate insurance coverage or directly by changing the incentives of medical care providers and the health insurance industry.

In the past, the government has selected a mix of health care policies. The Veterans Administration runs its own hospitals, hires its own physicians, and provides direct medical services. The Cost of Living Council experimented with health care cost controls in 1971–73, some of which may be reenacted under national health insurance. The Medicare program provides public insurance for the elderly, with half of the elderly supplementing this coverage with private insurance. Future health care programs are also unlikely to rely solely on any one approach.

Public versus Private Provision of Health Care

The choice of public or private provision of health care will depend on an assessment of whether a combination of incentives and regulatory requirements is sufficient to guarantee adequate performance from the private market or whether such performance can be obtained only through the public provision of services. Some argue that the helplessness of patients confronted by the complexities of modern medical technology is so pervasive and the economic self-interest of physicians so deeply entrenched that the consumer can be adequately protected only through public provision. Others favoring public provision feel that consumer preferences should not hold sway, even if it were possible to establish a system that would permit this. They argue that society as a whole shares the view that everyone should have exactly the same kind, amount, and quality of medical care and that provision through public hospitals and salaried physicians is the easiest method of achieving this goal.[34]

Proponents of private provision of medical care services rarely argue that the private market works well without any government intervention. As the previous sections have documented, there are many sources of failure in the private market. Rather, proponents of private provision believe that appropriate incentives and controls can be devised by government to curb the worst abuses of the private market and guarantee reasonable achievement of social goals. Even among those who are dubious that private provision can ever be reasonably successful, some favor trying further "patching up" of the present system rather than switching to a radically different method of providing care.

This is not equivalent to asserting that medical services should be dispensed on the basis of ability to pay. In fact, most of those who favor private provision also hold that there should be no substantial financial barriers to medical care. The elimination or reduction of payments made directly by patients, through insurance or governmental subsidy, is assumed, at least for those unable to afford needed care without assistance.

There are at least three reasons for the reluctance to abandon the private provision of medical services.

34. See, for example, Cotton M. Lindsay, "Medical Care and the Economics of Sharing," *Economica*, n.s. vol. 36 (November 1969), pp. 351–62.

The first is historical, reflecting the need to adopt a system that will be acceptable to those responsible for providing care. Physicians who have grown accustomed to considerable freedom in the conduct of their practices and to comfortable incomes are unlikely to welcome a major switchover to public provision. Without their cooperation, no plan is feasible.

The second reservation about public provision is the high cost of an extensive health program to the federal government. Recent experience in Great Britain has intensified a deep-seated concern about the adequacy of funding when the government must make choices among health care, other government goods and services, and lower taxes.[35] The British National Health Service is undergoing serious cuts in capital spending, at a time when waiting lists for some types of hospitalization have reached six years and when physicians are defecting to private agencies to regain their income position.

Finally, public provision would require extensive planning and administrative decisionmaking that could well be overwhelming in a large system of health care. Although other countries have tried public provision, none of their programs has approached the more than $100 billion undertaking required in the United States. Procedures would be required for determining how many hospital beds were needed where, how many physicians of what kind to train and hire, who should be hospitalized for what conditions and for how long, and what quality standards should be upheld. There is little indication that these decisions could be made better through a planned system than through automatic market incentives, with selected controls where necessary.

Health Insurance versus Subsidies to Suppliers

While there seems to be little interest in a switch to public provision of medical services, there is more active debate on the relative importance of subsidizing either those who purchase medical care or those who supply the care. Both approaches have been used extensively in the United States. Medicare and Medicaid finance medical services for the poor, disabled, and elderly regardless of where that care is rendered. Other programs, such as the neighborhood health centers, hospital construction under the Hill-Burton program, and the Comprehensive Health Man-

35. See Peter Mosley, "British National Health Plan 'Financially Undernourished'," *Washington Post,* July 6, 1974.

power Training Act, make payments to present or future providers of medical services.

The Nixon administration in 1973 urged greater concentration on consumer subsidies, through national health insurance, and reduced reliance on subsidies to the suppliers of specific services.[36] There are many reasons for this proposed switch in emphasis, ranging from the fragmentation and proliferation of supply programs that have made these programs difficult to administer effectively to the desire to give consumers wider freedom of choice in selecting a physician or a hospital.

Direct assistance to families and individuals is particularly appropriate under three circumstances: (1) when consumer choice and competition among suppliers seem desirable; (2) when it is in the public interest to increase the consumption of medical care as a whole rather than specific types of services such as polio immunizations; and (3) when public provision for particular groups will result in lower quality—for example, when the poor are segregated in separate facilities, such as charity hospitals.[37]

Subsidizing specific supply programs frequently results in a concentration of benefits on a small fraction of the needy population that is fortunate enough to live in a delimited geographical area. Thus, Chicanos who live within the census tracts defining the boundaries of the East Los Angeles Children and Youth project may receive comprehensive medical services of high quality, while those unfortunate enough to live just outside the boundaries may go without even basic care. Such programs could be expanded to cover all needy families, but they are rarely funded well enough for this. On the other hand, providing families with vouchers or insurance coverage makes it possible for them to obtain medical care whether or not their neighborhood has a governmentally funded health project.

Under some conditions, however, subsidies to suppliers can have distinct advantages. The major difficulty with providing assistance to families and individuals is that the market may respond to their enhanced purchasing power by charging higher prices, thus canceling out the benefits

36. See *Caspar W. Weinberger to be Secretary of Health, Education, and Welfare,* Hearings before the Senate Committee on Labor and Public Welfare, 93 Cong. 1 sess. (1973), pt. 2.

37. For an elaboration of these ideas, see Edward R. Fried and others, *Setting National Priorities: The 1974 Budget* (Brookings Institution, 1973), pp. 109–29, 184–91.

of the subsidy. This danger is less probable when services are provided in a competitive market with many alternative sources of care available to the public—a condition that is not characteristic of medical care services today. Unless policies are established to curb price increases, providing all Americans with health insurance is likely to be both costly and ineffective.

A similar problem is that even insured families and individuals may be unable to obtain care because of discrimination or a scarcity of medical resources. Institutional rigidities may prevent the market from responding to increased purchasing power for medical services for long periods of time. Subsidies to supply programs in communities with scarce medical resources, therefore, may be required to ensure the availability of medical services, even if consumers are widely subsidized. In order to provide medical services to all, some communities may also require other forms of assistance, such as improved transportation or other "outreach" services, which could be administered by supply programs for those who need them.

Subsidies to suppliers are particularly appropriate for making essential special services, such as certain types of immunization, available to all who require them. Health problems such as drug abuse, alcoholism, venereal disease, and mental illness may not receive adequate attention, even if those suffering from them are insured, unless patients have access to special centers that are known for their sympathetic treatment of these problems.

Subsidies to suppliers are also likely to be required to encourage the development of innovative methods of providing care. Institutional barriers may thwart the spontaneous development of alternative means of providing adequate quality care at lower cost by reducing the need for physicians' services, for example. Thus, the extensive use of paramedical personnel or the growth of organizations relying on such personnel may be minimal without developmental programs sponsored by the government.

In summary, providing assistance to individuals to help them meet medical expenses is generally preferable to subsidizing the suppliers of medical services. This assistance must be supplemented with subsidized supply programs, however, in the following circumstances: (1) when increased demand will dramatically drive up the prices of particular services or induce more costly methods of treatment; (2) when discrimination, scarcity of medical resources, or special difficulties in obtaining care prevent families from making effective use of health insurance; (3) when the social benefits of particular types of medical services are so significant that specific promotion of their use is called for; and (4) when necessary to encourage the development of innovative methods of providing care.

Private Insurance versus Public Insurance

If a decision is made to attack the nation's health care problems by providing increased direct assistance to families and individuals, this assistance could take many forms, ranging from tax subsidies that encourage the purchase of private insurance to the provision of comprehensive public insurance.

Administratively, tax subsidies are perhaps the easiest method of financing medical care. They can be used to reimburse families or individuals for medical expenses or for the purchase of "standard" insurance to pay those expenses. If tax subsidies take the form of deductions, as is the current practice, they have the greatest value for those with the highest incomes and the highest marginal tax rates. If the tax subsidies are in the form of tax credits, however, they can easily be focused on lower-income people, particularly if the tax credit is refundable even to those without any tax liability. The major disadvantages of the tax credit approach are that it provides no control over the cost or quality of care, and since it simply results in forgone government revenues, tax subsidies are automatic and not subject to annual congressional approval.

Rather than providing incentives through the tax system for individuals to purchase private insurance, the government could simply mandate that employers provide "standard" insurance to all employees. In reality, this compulsory premium contribution would be the same as a tax imposed on employers. In fact, if a firm were to respond to this premium by lowering wages or raising them less than it would otherwise, the premium would be borne by the employees. In this case, it would become a regressive tax, particularly if the premium were the same for everyone, hence representing a much higher share of income for low-income groups.

The only case in which an employer could not shift the cost of the premium to employees would be when wages were already at the minimum-wage level. For employers paying low wages, the premium would represent an increase in the minimum wage and would raise the firm's labor costs. A substantial cost increase would mean that some of these employers would have to go out of business or substantially reduce their labor force.

Mandating private insurance has the advantage of lowering the cost of insurance to the federal government, but at the same time it permits less control over the level of premiums or over the policies of insurance companies. Thus, it becomes difficult to overcome the natural tendency of the market to exclude bad risks and to rate groups on the basis of claims experience.

On the other hand, public provision of the minimum necessary insurance required to meet social goals is likely to result in lower administrative costs (both because economies of size can be realized and because marketing and selling costs can be avoided) and in better control over what is to be offered and who is to be covered. Less regressive methods of financing are also possible in a public plan, either through the payroll tax or through general revenues. One disadvantage of eliminating premiums as a method of financing, however, is that contributions to the cost of the plan no longer necessarily bear any relationship to the costs or amounts of services used. Thus, certain areas of the country with low medical prices and limited medical resources may be required to pay for medical care rendered in other areas.

At the end of the spectrum of possible alternative ways of subsidizing consumers is comprehensive public insurance, with virtually all medical care financed through a public plan. This would have many of the same disadvantages as public provision of medical services, since it would require large budgetary outlays and extensive administrative control over all major aspects of health care provision. In the absence of public provision, however, these controls would have to be designed to gain the cooperation of private providers and might be more difficult to administer and more costly than in a totally public system.

chapter three **The Current Mix of Private and Public Insurance**

The current mix of private and public health programs provides medical care and limits the financial burden of large medical expenditures for many Americans. Almost 80 percent of the population under 65 years of age has some hospitalization insurance and about the same percentage has surgical insurance. Nearly all the elderly and many of the permanently disabled are covered by Medicare. The federal-state Medicaid program in 1973 paid for medical care services received by more than 23 million low-income people. An examination of public and private health programs, however, reveals many serious gaps in coverage, despite extensive enrollment in private plans and sizable public expenditures.

Medical Expenditures and Third-Party Payments

Health care has grown from a $10 billion industry in 1950 to over $80 billion in 1973 (see Table 3-1). This eight-fold increase in expenditures for personal health care has been accompanied by even faster growth both in private insurance coverage and in public programs to assist certain groups in meeting their medical bills. Government expenditures at all levels increased from $2 billion in 1950 to $30 billion in 1973, with most of the growth following the introduction of the Medicare and Medicaid programs in 1966. Private health insurance has advanced from an infant industry paying out less than a billion dollars in benefits in 1950 to benefit payments of $20 billion in 1973.

As a result of these major trends, the share of health care expenses paid directly by patients declined from 68 percent in 1950 to 35 percent in 1973. Some services, however, are covered by third-party payers much

Table 3-1. Distribution of Personal Health Care Expenditures, by Source of Funds, Selected Fiscal Years, 1950–73

			Private		
Fiscal year	Total	Public	Direct payments by patients	Insurance benefits	Philanthropy and industry
		Aggregate amount (millions of dollars)			
1950	10,400	2,102	7,107	879	312
1960	22,729	4,930	12,576	4,698	525
1965	33,498	6,958	17,577	8,280	683
1970	59,127	20,550	23,281	14,406	890
1973	80,048	30,335	28,127	20,463	1,123
		Percentage distribution			
1950	100.0	20.2	68.3	8.5	3.0
1960	100.0	21.7	55.3	20.7	2.3
1965	100.0	20.8	52.5	24.7	2.0
1970	100.0	34.8	39.4	24.4	1.5
1973	100.0	37.9	35.1	25.6	1.4

Source: Barbara S. Cooper, Nancy L. Worthington, and Paula A. Piro, "National Health Expenditures, 1929–73," *Social Security Bulletin*, vol. 37 (February 1974), table 6, p. 15. Figures are rounded.

more extensively than others. Coverage of hospital care is now so pervasive that only 10 percent of all hospital expenses are paid directly by patients (see Table 3-2). Over half of the costs of hospital care are paid by federal, state, and local governments, while most of the remainder is paid through private insurance. Physicians' services, on the other hand, are not as well covered by either public programs or private insurance. In 1973, patients paid 42 percent of their physician bills directly, while insurance picked up 35 percent and government paid 22 percent. Other services, such as dental care and prescription drugs, were paid for almost totally by patients (87 percent). Almost 60 percent of nursing-home care, however, was provided by public programs.

Public programs benefit primarily the elderly and the poor. In 1973, government paid for 65 percent of all health care received by people aged sixty-five years and over but only 28 percent of that received by younger people (see Table 3-3). Private insurance was much more common among those under sixty-five, paying 33 percent of all their health care expenses but only 6 percent of the elderly's. Since the elderly have much higher medical bills, however, the amount they paid directly still substantially exceeded that paid by younger patients—$311 per capita (or about $367 including Medicare premiums) and $112 respectively.

Table 3-2. Distribution of Personal Health Care Expenditures, by Source
of Funds and Type of Expenditure, Fiscal Year 1973

Type of expenditure	Total	Public	*Direct payments by patients*	*Insurance benefits*	*Philanthropy and industry*
					Private
	Aggregate amount (millions of dollars)				
Hospital care	36,200	19,249	3,591	12,892	468
Physicians' services	18,040	4,041	7,642	6,344	13
Dentists' services	5,385	288	4,688	409	...
Drugs and drug sundries	8,780	670	7,660	450	...
All other services[a]	11,643	6,087	4,546	368	642
Total	80,048	30,335	28,127	20,463	1,123
	Per capita amount (dollars)				
Hospital care	170	90	17	60	2
Physicians' services	85	19	36	30	...
Dentists' services	25	1	22	2	...
Drugs and drug sundries	41	3	36	2	...
All other services[a]	55	29	21	2	3
Total	375	142	132	96	5
	Percentage distribution				
Hospital care	100.0	53.2	9.9	35.6	1.3
Physicians' services	100.0	22.4	42.4	35.2	0.1
Dentists' services	100.0	5.3	87.1	7.6	...
Drugs and drug sundries	100.0	7.6	87.2	5.1	...
All other services[a]	100.0	52.3	39.0	3.2	5.5
Total	100.0	37.9	35.1	25.6	1.4

Source: Same as Table 3-1, table 5, p. 13. Figures are rounded.
a. Includes other professional services, eyeglasses and appliances, nursing-home care, and services not elsewhere classified.

These trends and averages, however, conceal many important deficiencies in private and public coverage. Although only 10 percent of the cost
of hospital care is paid by patients, it makes a great deal of difference
whether this is due to all patients paying that percentage of their bill or
to some patients paying all the bill and others none. If many lower-
income families or families with extremely large hospital bills must pay
the entire bill, substantial financial hardship may be incurred. It is important, therefore, to explore in greater detail what kinds of people have
private insurance coverage and how comprehensive that coverage is, as
well as who benefits from public programs and any significant deficiencies in those programs.

Table 3-3. Distribution of Personal Health Care Expenditures, by Source of Funds and Age Groups, Fiscal Years 1966 and 1973

Fiscal year and age group	Total	Public	Private		
			Direct payments by patients	Insurance benefits	Philanthropy and industry
			Per capita amount (dollars)		
1966					
Under sixty-five	155	30	79	42	3
Sixty-five and over	445	133	237	71	5
1973					
Under sixty-five	300	83	112	100	5
Sixty-five and over	1,052	679	311[a]	58	5
			Percentage distribution		
1966					
Under sixty-five	100.0	19.4	51.1	27.3	2.2
Sixty-five and over	100.0	29.8	53.2	15.9	1.1
1973					
Under sixty-five	100.0	27.5	37.3	33.4	1.8
Sixty-five and over	100.0	64.5	29.6[a]	5.5	0.4

Source: Barbara S. Cooper and Paula A. Piro, "Age Differences in Medical Care Spending, Fiscal Year 1973," *Social Security Bulletin*, vol. 37 (May 1974), p. 13. Figures are rounded.

a. Direct payments by patients do not include Medicare premiums (which averaged $56 per elderly person in 1973). If these are classified as private payments, the public share would be reduced to 59.2 percent.

Private Health Insurance

Insurance coverage is most extensive for services provided inside the hospital. As shown in Table 3-4, 80 percent of the population under sixty-five has some private health insurance for hospital care, and almost that many have coverage for surgical physicians' services, in-hospital physician visits, and X-ray and laboratory examinations. Coverage of out-of-hospital services is less common. Less than half of the population under sixty-five has any insurance coverage for visits to a physician's office— whether for a physical check-up or for the treatment of chronic or acute illness. Fifty-five to 60 percent of the population under sixty-five is insured against the cost of prescribed drugs and private-duty nursing, but only 22 percent are insured against nursing-home care and less than 10 percent for dental services—even though both of these types of expenses can represent large out-of-pocket outlays.

While only 20 percent of the population under sixty-five has no private hospital insurance, a disproportionate number of the working poor, of

Table 3-4. Percentage of the Population Covered by Private Health Insurance Plans, by Age Group and Type of Service, December 31, 1972

Type of service	All ages	Under 65	65 and over
Hospital care	77.0	79.7	53.2
Physicians' services			
Surgical	74.0	77.1	46.3
In-hospital visits	72.2	76.1	38.5
X-ray and laboratory examinations	72.1	76.1	36.6
Office and home visits	48.2	51.3	20.5
Dental care	8.6	9.5	1.4
Prescribed drugs (out-of-hospital)	53.7	58.0	16.6
Private-duty nursing	52.6	56.7	16.3
Visiting-nurse service	55.9	59.9	21.2
Nursing-home care	21.9	21.5	25.8

Source: Marjorie S. Mueller, "Private Health Insurance in 1972: Health Care Services, Enrollment, and Finances," *Social Security Bulletin*, vol. 37 (February 1974), table 1, p. 21.

blacks, and of people living in the South are among those uninsured. So are people regarded by insurance companies as health risks. Forty percent of all black people under sixty-five and 75 percent of poor children do not have hospital insurance coverage (see Table 3-5). Of people under the age of sixty-five, 82 percent have insurance coverage in the Northeast compared with only 72 percent in the South. Health interview surveys show that "poor persons in the South are even less likely to have insurance than the poor in other regions."[1] Insurance coverage among farm residents is also low, with 40 percent uninsured for hospital expenses.

Private health insurance coverage among the working population depends crucially on the type of job held. Full-time workers are far more likely to have some private health insurance coverage than part-time workers or those without jobs. Table 3-6 shows that 88 percent of full-time workers have private insurance, but that only 44 percent of part-time workers and 27 percent of the unemployed have it. Furthermore, for any given type of worker, private insurance coverage is much more prevalent among higher-income workers. Thus only 41 percent of poor full-time workers have any health insurance, and less than 10 percent have coverage for care in a physician's office.

1. Edward B. Perrin, testimony in *National Health Insurance—Implications*, Hearings before the Subcommittee on Public Health and Environment of the House Committee on Interstate and Foreign Commerce, 93 Cong. 1 sess., 2 sess. (1974), p. 336.

National Health Insurance

Table 3-5. Percentage of the Population Covered by Private Hospital Insurance Plans, by Selected Characteristics, 1970

	Age group			
Characteristic	*Under 65*	*Under 17*	*17–44*	*45–64*
Total population	77.8	74.4	78.7	81.6
Annual income class (dollars)				
Under 3,000	39.3	25.4	49.0	41.7
3,000–4,999	53.1	41.7	56.3	67.2
5,000–9,999	80.3	77.3	80.0	86.6
10,000–14,999	90.1	89.1	89.5	93.1
15,000 and over	90.2	90.4	88.9	92.0
Race				
White	80.4	78.2	81.0	83.3
All other	59.9	53.7	65.0	65.2
Region				
Northeast	81.7	78.6	82.0	86.0
North Central	84.0	81.9	84.7	86.2
South	71.6	67.5	73.8	74.5
West	73.6	68.9	73.8	80.5
Area of residence[a]				
SMSA	81.3	78.2	82.2	84.6
Outside SMSA				
Nonfarm	74.4	71.0	76.4	76.9
Farm	61.9	59.7	62.3	64.7

Sources: Edward B. Perrin, testimony in *National Health Insurance—Implications*, Hearings before the Subcommittee on Public Health and Environment of the House Committee on Interstate and Foreign Commerce, 93 Cong. 1 sess., 2 sess. (1974), tables 2, 3, 5, pp. 342–44; and U.S. Department of Health, Education, and Welfare, Health Services and Mental Health Administration, *Age Patterns in Medical Care, Illness, and Disability, United States, 1968–1969* (1972), table N, p. 18.
SMSA: standard metropolitan statistical area.
a. Data are for 1968.

Coverage under employer group health insurance plans is also influenced by type of employment, as well as by sex, race, income, and other factors. For example, group insurance coverage ranges from 20 percent of full-time workers in agriculture to 92 percent in the communications and public utilities industry and averages 70 percent for all full-time workers (Table 3-7). Group insurance is somewhat more common among blue-collar workers than among white-collar workers, in part because many of the latter are self-employed, but coverage is lowest among service workers (52 percent) and farm workers (17 percent). Men are more likely to have group coverage than women, and middle-aged workers are more likely to have it than younger or older workers (Table

Table 3-6. **Private Health Insurance Enrollment Rates of People under Sixty-five Not Covered by Medicaid, by Labor Force Status of Family Head and Income Class, 1970**
Percent

		Annual income class (dollars)			
Labor force status of family head	All incomes	Poor (under 3,000)	Near poor (3,000– 5,000)	Middle income (7,000– 10,000)	High income (over 15,000)
		All private health insurance			
All family heads	76	38	65	92	95
Employed full time	88	41	73	89	98
Employed part time	44	35	52	62	...
Disabled[a]	38	20	41	...	...
Unemployed	27	4	20	...	...
		Insurance covering visits to physicians' offices			
All family heads	32	11	23	39	45
Employed full time	47	8	21	38	50
Employed part time	18	11	23	24	...
Disabled[a]	15	1	22	...	...
Unemployed	6	3	1	...	...

Source: Charles E. Phelps, testimony in *National Health Insurance—Implications*, Hearings, tables 6, 7, p. 361.
a. Many of the disabled counted in these statistics are now covered by Medicare.

3-8). Seventy-one percent of full-time working whites have group coverage compared with 65 percent of blacks and other minorities. Fifty-nine percent of full-time workers earning less than $5,000 have group coverage compared with 92 percent of those earning above $10,000. Regional patterns are also noticeable: 65 percent of full-time workers in the South have group coverage and 75 percent in the Northeast. Those who have been on the job for short periods of time or who work for small firms have particularly low levels of group coverage. Only about half of such workers are in group plans.

If workers are unable to be covered under a group insurance plan, they have few attractive alternatives. They must either buy insurance at high individual rates or be without coverage. A worker who has a wide range of jobs to choose from may be able to find a firm offering a good health insurance plan. For many workers, however, this is not a realistic option.

Private insurance, whether for groups or individuals, also frequently fails to cover large medical expenses. Only half of the population has any major medical insurance, and insurance companies often place limits on

38   National Health Insurance

Table 3-7. Percentage of Full-Time Workers Covered by Group Health Insurance,
by Industry and Occupation, April 1972

Industry and occupation	Total[a]	Covered	Not covered
All workers	100	70	29
Industry			
Agriculture	100	20	79
Mining	100	88	11
Construction	100	58	41
Manufacturing, durable goods	100	89	10
Manufacturing, nondurable goods	100	84	16
Transportation	100	79	21
Communications and public utilities	100	92	8
Trade, wholesale	100	75	24
Trade, retail	100	54	45
Finance, insurance, and real estate	100	75	24
Services	100	65	34
Occupation			
White-collar workers			
Professional and technical	100	77	22
Managers and officials	100	69	30
Sales	100	62	37
Clerical	100	74	25
Blue-collar workers			
Craftsmen	100	76	24
Operatives and kindred workers	100	80	19
Transport equipment operators	100	74	25
Nonfarm laborers	100	67	32
Service workers	100	52	47
Farm workers	100	17	81

Source: Walter W. Kolodrubetz, "Group Health Insurance Coverage of Full-Time Employees, 1972," *Social Security Bulletin*, vol. 37 (April 1974), tables 2, 4, pp. 19, 22. Figures are rounded.
a. Includes nonresponses not shown separately.

payments. Even policies for many high-wage firms have inadequate provisions, with maximum liabilities restricted to as little as $5,000. In low-wage industries, insurance benefits are more limited still. In one such industry, hospital benefits of only $15 a day for a maximum of thirty-one days are provided, and the most expensive surgical allowance is $250.[2] One-third of all private hospitalization plans are limited in coverage to sixty days or less. Thus, even workers with some private health insurance coverage may be bankrupted if they incur long hospitalization or high medical bills. In 1970, over 4 million Americans had out-of-pocket

2. U.S. Department of Health, Education, and Welfare, Fact Sheet Package, February 1974.

Table 3-8. Percentage of Full-Time Workers Covered by Group Health Insurance, by Selected Characteristics, April 1972

Characteristic	Total[a]	Covered	Not covered
All workers	100	70	29
Sex			
Male	100	74	25
Female	100	61	38
Age			
Under 25	100	62	37
25–44	100	74	26
45–64	100	71	29
65 and over	100	45	54
Race			
White	100	71	29
All other	100	65	34
Annual earnings (dollars)			
1–4,999	100	59	40
5,000–9,999	100	83	16
10,000–14,999	100	92	8
15,000 and over	100	92	8
Region			
Northeast	100	75	25
North Central	100	72	28
South	100	65	35
West	100	71	28
Size of firm (employees)			
Under 25	100	50	50
25–99	100	77	23
100 or more	100	90	10
Length of employment (months)			
Less than 3	100	42	57
3–6	100	50	49
6–9	100	61	38
9–12	100	64	35
12 or more	100	76	24

Source: Same as Table 3-7, tables 5–7, pp. 25–27, and tables 9–11, pp. 29–31. Figures are rounded.
a. Includes nonresponses, not shown separately.

medical expenses in excess of $1,000; almost 1 million of those were members of families with incomes below $5,000, and the families of another 1 million had incomes between $5,000 and $10,000.[3] While these

3. U.S. Department of Health, Education, and Welfare, National Center for Health Statistics, *Monthly Vital Statistics Report,* vol. 22, no. 1, Supplement (April 2, 1973), p. 6.

Table 3-9. Medicaid Payments and Number of Medicaid Recipients, Public Assistance Recipients, and Poor People, Fiscal Years 1967–73

Fiscal year	Medicaid payments		Medicaid recipients		Public assistance recipients		People below the low-income level	
	Amount[a] (millions of dollars)	Annual increase (percent)	Number (millions)	Annual increase (percent)	Number[b] (millions)	Annual increase (percent)	Number (millions)	Annual change (percent)
1967	2,475	…	9.5	…	8.1	…	27.8	…
1968	3,723	50.4	11.4	20.0	8.9	9.9	25.4	−8.6
1969	4,596	23.4	14.0	22.8	9.7	9.0	24.1	−5.1
1970	5,213	13.4	15.5	10.7	11.1	14.4	25.4	5.4
1971	6,278	20.4	19.3	24.5	13.8	24.3	25.6	0.8
1972	7,752	23.5	20.6	6.7	14.8	7.2	24.5	−4.3
1973	8,923	15.1	23.5	14.1	15.1	2.0	23.0	−6.1
Average change, 1967–73	…	24.4	…	16.5	…	11.1	…	−3.0

Sources: Medicaid payments—1967–70, U.S. Social Security Administration, *Compendium of National Health Expenditures Data*, DHEW (SSA) 73-11903 (n.d.), table 8, pp. 53–56; 1971–73, Cooper and others, "National Health Expenditures, 1929–73," table 3, pp. 8–10. Medicaid recipients—1970–71, U.S. Department of Health, Education, and Welfare, National Center for Social Statistics, *Medicaid and Other Medical Care Financed from Public Assistance Funds, Fiscal Year 1971*, NCSS Report B-5 (FY 71) (1972), p. 1; 1967–69, estimated from monthly data in NCSS Report B-5, 1968 and 1969 issues; 1972–73, *Special Analyses, Budget of the United States Government, Fiscal Year 1974*, p. 150, and *Fiscal Year 1975*, p. 149. Public assistance recipients—*Social Security Bulletin* (February 1974), table M-25, p. 69. People below the low-income level—1967–72, U.S. Bureau of the Census, *Current Population Reports*, Series P-60, No. 91, "Characteristics of the Low-Income Population, 1972" (1973), table 1, p. 15; 1973, *Current Population Reports*, Series P-60, No. 96, "Household Money Income in 1973 and Selected Social and Economic Characteristics of Households" (1974), table 1, p. 4.
n.a. Not available.
a. Payments to medical vendors for services to Medicaid and other public assistance recipients.
b. As of December, the midpoint of the fiscal year.

2 million people for whom medical expenses are a heavy financial burden represent only 1 percent of the total population, for them and their families the inadequacy of present programs is a serious problem.

Medicaid

Many poor people were without needed care before the introduction of the federal-state Medicaid program. Medicaid attempted to alleviate this situation—if not for all the poor, at least for those on welfare. Half the states also provide coverage to the "medically needy," who might be forced onto the welfare rolls if they attempted to meet their medical bills directly.[4]

Under Medicaid, the federal government shares with the states the costs of providing many different kinds of medical services. The federal share of costs ranges from 83 percent in the lowest-income states to 50 percent in high-income states—for example, New York, California, and Massachusetts. Each state determines eligibility based on income and asset requirements that vary widely. Medicaid tries to encourage uniform benefits among the states by requiring coverage for such basic services as hospital care and physician services. The coverage of other items—drugs, dental services, optometrist services, private nurses, and so forth—is optional. Some states have added the full range of optional services, but others cover only a few. In addition, the states are permitted to place limits on the extent of the coverage of basic services; for example, one state (Louisiana) covers only fifteen days of hospital care, and other states place limits on the number of physician visits. Nearly all states purchase Medicare physician insurance for elderly welfare recipients and pay the patient's share of Medicare costs.

Medicaid Experience

Medicaid expenditures have increased rapidly since the program's inception, from $2.5 billion in fiscal year 1967 to $9 billion in 1973, or by an average of almost 25 percent a year (see Table 3-9). During that

4. Medically needy people eligible for Medicaid are individuals who are aged, blind, or disabled, or families with dependent children whose income net of medical expense is within 133 percent of the public assistance support level.

same period, the number of people receiving Medicaid benefits rose from just under 10 million in 1967 to 23.5 million in 1973—increasing by almost 17 percent each year. But these were years of rapid growth in the welfare rolls as well: public assistance recipients increased from 8 million in 1967 to 15 million in 1973. Although the number of recipients of Medicaid benefits grew primarily because the welfare rolls were increasing, it is also true that some growth occurred because more people were brought into the program as medically needy and because more of those eligible for benefits actually received medical care services. Despite this increase in numbers, the average annual payment to each recipient of Medicaid benefits—about $330—remained virtually unchanged between 1968 and 1971. Only in very recent years has there been any substantial increase in the average payment. During much of the period that Medicaid has been in operation, however, benefits per person have declined in real terms.

State governments have reacted with alarm to their share of the rapidly accelerating cost of the program and have taken steps to restrict benefits to the poor and payments to medical providers. These actions in turn have contributed to the inability of the program to live up to the high expectations both of those with low incomes who hoped to receive high-quality medical care and of those hoping to receive suitable compensation for providing such care to the poor. Thus, Medicaid has wound up costing more than anticipated and falling short of providing expected benefits.

Impact on Use of Medical Services by the Poor

Concern with costs and disappointment with Medicaid, however, have obscured the genuine accomplishments of the program. Medicaid has reached large numbers of the poor, and recent evidence indicates that there has been a marked improvement in the amount of medical care received by the poor. In 1970, 65 percent of the low-income population saw a physician during the year; only 56 percent had done so in 1963.[5] Furthermore, this increase did not occur for the higher-income groups so that the poor proportionately increased their use of services in relation to

5. In 1963, families with incomes below $4,000 were classified as low-income; in 1970, those with incomes below $6,000 (Ronald Andersen and others, *Health Services Use: National Trends and Variations, 1953–1971*, DHEW [HSM] 73-3004, Department of Health, Education, and Welfare, Health Services and Mental Health Administration [1972], p. 9).

Table 3-10. Visits to Physicians per Capita, by Age Group and Family Income Class, 1964 and 1971

Age group and income class[a]	1964	1971
All ages	4.5	4.9
Low income	4.3	5.6
Middle income	4.5	4.7
High income	4.9	4.9
Ratio, high income to low income	1.1	0.9
Under 15		
Low income	2.7	4.0
Middle income	3.8	4.1
High income	4.5	4.8
Ratio, high income to low income	1.7	1.2
15–64		
Low income	4.5	5.8
Middle income	4.7	4.9
High income	4.9	4.8
Ratio, high income to low income	1.1	0.8
65 and over		
Low income	6.3	6.7
Middle income	7.0	6.4
High income	7.3	7.5
Ratio, high income to low income	1.2	1.1

Sources: 1964, U.S. Department of Health, Education, and Welfare, National Center for Health Statistics, *Volume of Physician Visits by Place of Visit and Type of Service, United States—July 1963–June 1964*, Series 10, No. 18 (1965), pp. 19, 29; 1971, unpublished tabulations provided by NCHS.

a. Low income is defined as under $4,000 in 1964 and under $5,000 in 1971; middle income as $4,000–$6,999 in 1964 and $5,000–$9,999 in 1971; high income as $7,000 and above in 1964 and $10,000 and above in 1971.

others. As shown in Table 3-10, in 1964, before Medicaid started, people with high incomes visited physicians 15 percent more frequently than those with low incomes. By 1971, people in the low-income group exceeded those in other income groups in the average number of times they visited their physicians. Pregnant women among the poor also began to visit physicians earlier: 71 percent of low-income women who delivered live babies received medical attention in the first trimester of pregnancy in 1970 compared with only 58 percent in 1963.[6]

While these trends suggest that Medicaid has been largely successful in helping those who are covered to receive medical services, several qualifications must be made.

First, it should be noted that Medicaid does not provide medical care

6. Ibid., p. 22.

services for all poor people but only for those falling within certain welfare categories, such as single-parent families, the blind, the disabled, and
the aged. In 1973, an estimated 23.5 million people received Medicaid
services. The Council of Economic Advisers has estimated that 30 percent of all Medicaid recipients are above the official poverty level,[7] so
only 16.5 million of the Medicaid recipients are poor. About 6.5 million
poor people, or 28 percent of the poor, are without financial assistance
from Medicaid for medical services. Those who are excluded from
Medicaid continue to lag well behind other poor people and higher-
income people in their use of medical services.[8]

A second important qualification is that the poor have more severe
health problems than higher-income people. Once adjustment is made for
the greater health problems of the poor, the use of medical services increases uniformly with income. The poor who are eligible for welfare use
physician services about the same as middle-income people with comparable health problems, while those in the low-income group who are
not on public assistance lag substantially behind others in their use of
services. Children in families with incomes above $15,000 visit physicians
53 percent more frequently than poor children who are not on welfare,
while high-income elderly people see physicians 72 percent more often
than poor elderly people who are not on welfare but have the same health
problems.[9]

Third, even though the poor have made rapid gains in the number of
medical services received, they do not participate in "mainstream" medicine of comparable quality and convenience to that received by the more
fortunate. Instead, the poor—whether on welfare or not—are much more
likely to receive care from general practitioners rather than specialists, in
a hospital outpatient department rather than in a physician's office, and
after traveling long distances and waiting substantially longer for care.[10]

Finally, even among those covered by Medicaid, benefits vary widely
by type of medical service, by basis of eligibility, by geographical area,
and by race.

7. *Economic Report of the President, February 1974,* table 45, p. 168.
8. See Karen Davis and Roger Reynolds, "The Impact of Medicare and Medicaid on Access to Medical Care," in Richard N. Rosett (ed.), *The Role of Health
Insurance in the Health Services Sector,* A Conference of the Universities–National Bureau Committee for Economic Research (National Bureau of Economic
Research, 1975).
9. For documentation, see ibid.
10. See ibid.

Composition of Medicaid Payments by Medical
Service and Basis of Eligibility

About 65 percent of all Medicaid expenditures goes for institutional care in hospitals or nursing homes. Less than 20 percent goes for physician services either in private practice or in hospital outpatient facilities. The remainder is for drugs, dental care, and other optional services. Nursing-home care is a major source of Medicaid expenditures. While only 3 percent of Medicaid recipients receive nursing-home services, payments for them account for 23 percent of all Medicaid payments, with an average annual payment of over $2,500.

The emphasis on institutional care in the Medicaid program is reflected in the distribution of payments among those eligible. The aged, blind, and disabled represent only 28 percent of Medicaid recipients but account for 53 percent of Medicaid payments. Even though children represent almost half of the poor and 45 percent of Medicaid recipients, they receive only 18 percent of the payments.

Only in recent years has an attempt been made to stress preventive care for younger people. The early diagnosis, screening, and treatment program for children was delayed for a number of years for lack of federal regulations. Now all Medicaid states are required to seek out eligible children and provide such care for them. Enforcement of this requirement, however, has not been vigorous to date.

Geographical Variation in Medicaid Benefits

Because the states have considerable leeway in setting eligibility requirements and benefit coverage, some states have far more generous programs than others. In fiscal 1972, Medicaid payments per recipient averaged $292 in southern states and $511 in the Northeast region. While part of this difference reflects lower medical costs in the South, there remains a considerable variation in real benefits.

An even greater source of variation in the program is the extent to which different states cover all of the poor. The ratio of Medicaid recipients to the total poor population is 1.03 in the Northeast and 1.16 in the West, suggesting that in those areas nearly all of the poor, and probably many near-poor people as well, are receiving benefits. In the South, however, there are less than one-third as many Medicaid recipients as there are poor people. Thus, the South, with 46 percent of the poor population, has only 20 percent of Medicaid recipients and 17 percent of Medicaid payments. Payments per poor person range from $85 annually in the South to $526 in the Northeast.

Because the program concentrates on the older population and on such benefits as nursing-home services, children are even less well covered. Medicaid payments per child recipient averaged $43 in Mississippi compared with $133 in New York (Table 3-11). Moreover, only one-tenth of the poor children in Mississippi received Medicaid benefits whereas nearly all the poor and many of the near-poor children in New York received them. As a consequence, the disparity in payments per poor child was even larger.

Since Medicaid benefits go predominantly to families headed by nonworking women and many of the rural poor are families with unemployed or underemployed fathers, few children in rural families receive benefits. In Table 3-12, average Medicaid expenditures per poor child in rural areas are shown to be about $5 annually, compared with $76 in central cities. Urban-rural differences also exist for other age groups: benefits for the elderly poor in central cities are twice that in rural areas.

Lower Medicaid benefits for rural families are undoubtedly a product of the urban focus of the program. In addition, the poor in urban communities are better organized and more informed about eligibility for assistance. The lower benefits received by rural residents also reflect the scarcity of medical resources, particularly physicians and nursing-home care, in those areas. While the poor as a whole have markedly increased their use of physicians' services since the introduction of Medicaid, rural residents have not made any gains relative to urban areas in use of medical services. Medicaid, therefore, has probably failed to meet the needs of large numbers of poor people outside of urban areas.

Race and Medicaid Benefits

There are also wide variations in Medicaid benefits on the basis of race. White Medicaid recipients average 75 percent higher payments than black Medicaid recipients (Table 3-13). Poor blacks are somewhat more likely to be eligible for Medicaid, however, particularly in the urban, northern states. Thus, seven out of ten poor blacks receive Medicaid services compared with slightly more than half of poor whites. Medicaid payments per poor white person, therefore, are 36 percent higher than average payments per poor black person.

For those eligible for Medicaid, disparity in benefits is particularly marked for nursing-home care. Whites receive five times the nursing-home payments received by blacks (Table 3-14). Hearings of the House Committee on the Judiciary indicate that substantial discrimination, both overt and institutional, exists in nursing homes.[11] Institutional discrimination arises primarily from segregated housing patterns and the referral patterns of physicians, who refer patients to only some of all available nursing homes.

White Medicaid recipients also receive payments for private physicians' services that are 40 percent higher than those received by blacks, although this is offset in part by the greater use by blacks of hospital outpatient departments as a source of medical care. Overt discrimination by private physicians—such as segregated waiting rooms and longer waiting times for black patients—apparently still exists in a number of areas.[12] The Judiciary hearings also point to the importance of institutional factors, particularly the shortage of physicians in minority neighborhoods, that give rise to racial benefit patterns.[13]

Racial disparities are not greater in the South than in other regions but are much more pronounced in nonmetropolitan areas than in large cities. Whites average more than twice the payments for medical care of blacks in nonmetropolitan counties.

Medicare

The Medicare program for the elderly differs from Medicaid in that it is a federal program with uniform benefits. All elderly people covered by the social security program are automatically eligible for hospitalization insurance, and 96 percent of those with hospitalization insurance also enroll in the voluntary supplementary medical insurance plan (SMI)

11. *Title VI Enforcement in Medicare and Medicaid Programs,* Hearings before the Subcommittee on Civil Rights and Constitutional Rights of the House Committee on the Judiciary, 93 Cong. 1 sess. (1974), especially pp. 2–12. For a discussion of the different kinds of discrimination, see Ray Marshall, "The Economics of Racial Discrimination: A Survey," *Journal of Economic Literature,* vol. 12 (September 1974), pp. 849–71.

12. For a case study in one Alabama town, see the speech delivered by Melbah McAfee, at the conference, "Resolved: The South Will Feed Its Hungry," University of North Carolina, June 23, 1974; transcription.

13. See, for example, *Title VI Enforcement,* pp. 15, 18, 19.

Table 3-11. Medicaid Payments per Recipient and per Poor Person, and Ratio of Recipients to Poor, by Age and State, 1970

Payments in dollars

Region and state[a,b]	Children, under 21			Adults, 21–64			Adults, 65 and over		
	Medicaid payments per child recipient	Ratio of recipients to poor children	Medicaid payments per poor child	Medicaid payments per adult recipient	Ratio of recipients to poor adults	Medicaid payments per poor adult	Medicaid payments per aged recipient	Ratio of recipients to poor aged	Medicaid payments per poor aged
United States[a]	**126**	**0.55**	**69**	**408**	**0.61**	**250**	**527**	**0.69**	**363**
Northeast[a]	**132**	**1.24**	**163**	**404**	**1.31**	**530**	**999**	**0.67**	**667**
Maine	109	0.48	52	321	0.46	147	341	0.32	110
New Hampshire	98	0.46	45	471	0.37	174	150	0.52	78
Vermont	201	0.80	160	361	0.60	215	601	0.72	435
Rhode Island	134	0.72	97	354	1.02	362	633	1.30	825
Connecticut	149	1.04	155	674	0.53	359	1,803	0.51	918
New York	133	1.68	224	450	1.72	773	1,049	1.02	1,075
New Jersey	153	0.70	108	215	0.63	134	1,942	0.22	433
Pennsylvania	117	0.97	113	329	1.28	422	675	0.38	259
North Central	**137**	**0.49**	**67**	**525**	**0.41**	**216**	**700**	**0.40**	**279**
Ohio	103	0.40	41	435	0.36	156	629	0.29	185
Indiana	89	0.26	23	417	0.22	93	376	0.21	78
Illinois	159	0.70	111	558	0.50	279	546	0.34	185
Michigan	122	0.51	62	573	0.62	356	1,260	0.47	593
Wisconsin	237	0.66	155	848	0.47	395	1,054	0.62	656
Minnesota	143	0.72	103	607	0.40	243	1,044	0.55	573
Iowa	103	0.43	44	319	0.32	101	227	0.32	73
Missouri	80	0.33	26	331	0.33	110	296	0.55	161
North Dakota	142	0.20	29	587	0.22	127	928	0.40	367
South Dakota	114	0.14	17	440	0.14	62	690	0.28	196
Nebraska	120	0.31	38	492	0.31	154	382	0.39	150
Kansas	129	0.51	66	498	0.45	226	478	0.36	170

South[a]	**108**	**0.20**	**21**	**349**	**0.23**	**79**	**334**	**0.53**	**176**
Delaware	64	0.81	52	343	0.48	165	151	0.28	42
Maryland	118	0.73	86	376	0.83	313	464	0.68	316
District of Columbia	171	1.10	189	442	0.72	317	431	0.67	291
Virginia	98	0.20	19	374	0.18	69	250	0.28	69
West Virginia	87	0.38	33	183	0.39	71	135	0.19	25
South Carolina	65	0.09	6	325	0.19	60	475	0.38	180
Georgia	87	0.26	23	447	0.31	139	416	0.71	296
Florida	68	0.20	13	192	0.25	48	351	0.43	150
Kentucky	76	0.38	29	262	0.37	96	231	0.68	158
Tennessee	66	0.16	10	222	0.17	37	166	0.32	53
Alabama	97	0.10	10	446	0.11	48	511	0.49	253
Mississippi	43	0.11	5	264	0.07	20	181	0.49	89
Arkansas	56	0.06	4	179	0.10	17	68	0.19	13
Louisiana	112	0.08	9	260	0.18	46	245	0.94	230
Oklahoma	201	0.37	75	402	0.43	174	583	0.64	372
Texas	215	0.08	17	738	0.09	69	326	0.66	213
West[b]	**122**	**0.96**	**117**	**389**	**1.29**	**500**	**350**	**1.97**	**690**
Montana	127	0.28	35	451	0.26	118	669	0.31	207
Idaho	90	0.26	23	436	0.29	126	829	0.26	217
Wyoming	75	0.18	13	308	0.18	56	273	0.24	67
Colorado	91	0.40	36	340	0.55	186	328	1.34	440
New Mexico	97	0.26	25	352	0.29	103	274	0.37	101
Utah	190	0.27	52	329	0.73	240	376	0.50	186
Nevada	119	0.47	56	558	0.34	190	794	0.55	440
Washington	99	0.70	69	317	1.13	359	748	0.67	498
Oregon	99	0.35	35	283	0.47	133	298	0.31	92
California	126	1.33	168	389	1.73	672	321	3.17	1,017
Hawaii	100	0.92	92	319	1.01	322	1,162	0.96	1,119

Sources: Medicaid payments and recipients: U.S. Department of Health, Education, and Welfare, Social and Rehabilitation Service, "Numbers of Recipients and Amounts of Payments under Medicaid and Other Medical Programs Financed from Public Assistance Funds," DHEW Publication (SRS) 73-03153 (1972; processed); poverty population: U.S. Bureau of the Census, *Census of Population, 1970, Detailed Characteristics*, Series PC(1)-D, Tables 207, 215, 216.

a. Data not reported for Massachusetts and North Carolina. Regional and national totals do not include these states.

b. Arizona and Alaska did not have Medicaid programs in 1970. Regional and national totals do not include these states.

Table 3-12. Mean Expenditure for All Personal Health Services per Low-Income Person,[a] by Age Group and Area of Residence, 1970

Age group and area of residence	Total mean expenditure (dollars)	Mean expenditure paid by Medicaid and other free care (dollars)	Percent of total mean expenditure paid by Medicaid and other free care
Under 18			
SMSA, central city	101	76	75.2
Other urban	124	58	46.8
Rural	46	5	10.9
18–64			
SMSA, central city	360	158	43.9
Other urban	352	83	23.6
Rural	281	52	18.5
65 and over			
SMSA, central city	446	54	12.1
Other urban	329	38	11.6
Rural	407	27	6.6

Source: Ronald Andersen and others, *Expenditures for Personal Health Services: National Trends and Variations, 1953–1970*, DHEW (HRA) 74-3105, U.S. Department of Health, Education, and Welfare, Health Resources Administration (1973), table A-11, p. 52.

SMSA: standard metropolitan statistical area.

a. Low income is defined as having a family income below $6,000.

that covers physician services and provides certain other benefits. Recent amendments extend Medicare benefits to people with chronic kidney disease and also to some disabled persons under sixty-five.

Beneficiaries must pay a deductible of $92 (effective January 1, 1975), covering up to sixty days in the hospital; between the sixty-first and ninetieth days they must pay coinsurance of $23 a day; for the next sixty days they must pay $46 a day, after which hospital insurance ceases. Under SMI they must pay each year the first $60 of physician charges and 20 percent of the remainder. They also pay a monthly premium for SMI—set at $6.70, effective July 1, 1974. Federal expenditures under Medicare are expected to total $15 billion in fiscal 1976, covering medical care services for 24 million elderly, disabled, and chronically ill persons.[14]

Medicare has markedly increased the elderly's access to medical care services, particularly to institutional services such as hospital and nursing-home care. However, the program still has several shortcomings. Even

14. *Special Analyses, Budget of the United States Government, Fiscal Year 1976*, p. 183.

Table 3-13. Medicaid Payments per Recipient and per Poor Person and Ratios of Recipients to Poor, by Region and Race, 1969

Payments in dollars

Region of residence and race	Medicaid payments per recipient	Ratio of Medicaid recipients to poor people	Medicaid payments per poor person
United States[a]			
White	376	0.53	200
Other	213	0.69	147
Ratio, white to other	1.77	0.77 *23% more others*	1.36 *X more*
Northeast			
White	364	1.68	611
Other	205	1.95	399
Ratio, white to other	1.78	0.86 *14% more others*	1.53 *X more*
North Central			
White	447	0.33	146
Other	249	0.79	197
Ratio, white to other	1.79	0.41 *59% more others*	0.74
South			
White	322	0.26	85
Other	180	0.31	56
Ratio, white to other	1.79	0.85 *15% more others*	1.53 *X more*

Source: Unpublished state Medicaid reports. Figures are rounded.

a. Based on data for twenty-three states and the District of Columbia that had Medicaid programs in 1969. Northeast—Connecticut and New York; North Central—Idaho, Illinois, Iowa, Michigan, Minnesota, Missouri, North Dakota, Ohio, South Dakota, Wisconsin; South—Delaware, District of Columbia, Georgia, Kentucky, Louisiana, Maryland, Oklahoma, Texas; West—Montana, Nevada, New Mexico, Wyoming. Data for the West are not shown separately, since states there with significant numbers of blacks and other nonwhites did not report data by race.

though the same set of basic benefits is available to all covered persons regardless of income, race, or geographical location, there are wide differences in the use of services and in the benefits received by different groups. As is the case with Medicaid, the groups with the poorest health—blacks, rural residents, and people living in the South—receive the lowest benefits from the program.

Inequality by Income

Benefits from the physician portion of Medicare are particularly unequally distributed among income classes. Despite better health, the elderly whose family incomes are above $15,000 a year receive twice as much under Medicare's voluntary supplementary medical insurance program as those with incomes below $5,000. About half of this difference

Table 3-14. Medicaid Payments per Recipient, by Race, Type of Medical Service Received, Age, and Residence, 1969[a]

Payments in dollars

Characteristic of recipient	Payment per recipient		Ratio of payments, white to other
	White	Other	
All services	376	213	1.77
Type of medical service received[b]			
General hospital	110	102	1.08
Nursing home	129	26	5.01
Physicians' services	35	26	1.38
Hospital outpatient	11	17	0.67
Drugs	27	15	1.77
Age			
Under 21	130	117	1.11
21–64	447	341	1.31
65 and over	696	328	2.12
Area of residence			
SMSA, cities of 400,000 or more	333	221	1.51
Other SMSA	426	228	1.87
Outside SMSA	406	179	2.27

Sources: Karen Davis, "Financing Medical Care: Implications for Access to Primary Care," in Spyros Andreopoulos (ed.), *Primary Care: Where Medicine Fails* (Wiley, 1974), p. 172; and unpublished state Medicaid reports. The ratios are calculated from data before rounding.

SMSA: standard metropolitan statistical area.

a. Based on data from twenty-three states and the District of Columbia that had Medicaid programs in 1969 and reported data by race. Those reporting contained 72 percent of the total poor black population in all states with Medicaid programs.

b. Payments per recipient of any medical service, rather than per recipient of services covered by Medicaid only; for example, in the first column, payments to whites for general hospital services are divided by the total number of white Medicaid recipients.

is accounted for by differences in frequency of use, while the other half reflects the greater reliance on specialists and more expensive physicians by higher-income people. But these differences are not attributable solely to advantages that most higher-income persons possess, such as more education or living in areas with a greater concentration of specialized medical resources. In fact, the $60 deductible and 20 percent coinsurance provisions of the physician portion of Medicare constitute significant deterrents to the use of medical services by the poor. Thus, for the low-income people for whom Medicaid pays the premium, deductible, and coinsurance required by Medicare, use of medical services is commensurate with that of middle-income persons having similar health problems.[15]

15. For further elaboration and documentation of the impact of Medicare discussed in this section, see Davis and Reynolds, "The Impact of Medicare and Medicaid on Access to Medical Care."

For poor people not covered by Medicaid, use of medical services lags substantially behind that of higher-income people with similar health conditions.

Inequality by Race

There are also substantial inequalities in Medicare benefits on the basis of race. Medicare has contributed to the reduction of racial barriers to medical care through its insistence that hospitals provide services on a nondiscriminatory basis as a prerequisite for participation in the Medicare program. However, despite notable achievements in access to hospital care for minorities, the program has not been very successful in ensuring equality in treatment for other types of medical services, particularly physician and nursing-home services. In 1968, Medicare payments per person enrolled were 30 percent more for inpatient hospital care for elderly whites than for blacks, 60 percent more for physician services, and more than twice as much for extended care facility service. In the South, the racial disparity is greater: whites received 55 percent more for inpatient hospital care, 95 percent more for physician services, and almost two and one-half times as much for extended care services. Furthermore, the lower utilization of medical services by blacks is attributable not only to their lower average incomes and poorer education, but to discrimination and other factors associated with race.[16] The unequal access of elderly blacks to these services is particularly regrettable in view of their generally poorer health and limited supporting services in the home.

If national health insurance is to provide equal access to medical care for blacks and other minorities, nondiscriminatory practices by providers of medical services must be rigorously enforced. In addition, programs specifically designed to increase the access of minorities to medical care are essential.

Regional Disparities

Despite the national uniformity policy of the Medicare program, there are substantial variations in benefits by location. Elderly people in the West, for example, receive 45 percent more in Medicare payments per

16. See ibid.

person enrolled than the elderly in the South. About one-fourth of this difference is accounted for by regional medical price differences, while the rest reflects the lower utilization of medical services by the elderly in areas with few medical resources per capita.[17] Urban-rural differences are similar. Those eligible for Medicare benefits in nonmetropolitan counties received $280 per person in 1971, compared with $395 for those in metropolitan counties.[18] Again, if national health insurance is to provide an equitable distribution of benefits, specific programs to improve the delivery of health care services in rural areas and areas with limited medical resources must be developed.

Incomplete Coverage

Since Medicare is restricted to people covered by social security and the railroad retirement system, several hundred thousand of the elderly are not automatically eligible to receive benefits. In 1972, Medicare was amended to permit those elderly people not covered by social security to purchase Medicare hospitalization insurance at a premium sufficient to cover the average cost of the program—about $400 annually. But since some of those excluded from coverage, such as former domestic workers or migrant laborers, are very poor, this change is of only limited benefit. Furthermore, the $80 premium charged for coverage under the physician portion of Medicare has effectively deterred about three-quarters of a million elderly people from receiving that coverage; and, once again, the poor, blacks, and people living in the South are disproportionately represented among the excluded.

Inadequate Catastrophic Coverage

Although Medicare meets a large portion of medical bills for many of the elderly, it nevertheless subjects all covered persons to the possibility of burdensome out-of-pocket expenditures. Under the hospital insurance plan, once the patient has been in the hospital for 150 days the program

17. U.S. Social Security Administration, Office of Research and Statistics, *Medicare: Health Insurance for the Aged, 1968*, Sec. 1, *Summary* (1973), table 1.6, p. 1–7, and p. xxiv.
18. U.S. Social Security Administration, Office of Research and Statistics, *Medicare: Health Insurance for the Aged: Amounts Reimbursed, by State and County, 1971*, DHEW (SSA) 73-11704 (n.d.), p. 48.

makes no further payments and the patient is forced to pick up all expenses.[19] Even a patient hospitalized for 150 days would be required to pay over $3,000.

The physician portion of Medicare, while placing no limits on the amounts covered, pays only 80 percent of "allowable" physician charges. The patient must pay the first $60 of bills, the other 20 percent of the "allowable" fee, and any excess over the allowable amount. Other services such as private-duty nursing and out-of-hospital drugs are not covered at all. If an elderly person is sick long enough, he or she may incur ruinous out-of-pocket costs.

19. Coverage is limited to 90 days plus a lifetime reserve of 60 days.

chapter four **Basic Issues in National Health Insurance**

Evaluating the possible alternative approaches to national health insurance requires decisions about a multitude of issues. A plan must be designed so that it not only meets today's needs but also is flexible enough to adjust to the demands of changing medical technology. Deciding which of the many possible features of a national health insurance plan should be included is not always a clear-cut choice. In most cases, some trade-off must be made between one set of advantages and another. An attempt is made in this chapter to clarify the trade-offs involved in most of the major features of national health insurance plans.

Who Should Be Covered?

The first choice to be made in designing a national health insurance plan is the extent of population coverage. National health insurance aims primarily at assisting people with low incomes or high medical bills; yet a national health insurance plan that attempts to meet only their needs may fail to do so. Demands on the medical care system by higher-income people who are excluded from the plan but covered under private insurance may divert resources away from the poor. Physicians may find treatment of higher-income patients financially more attractive than serving the poor, and subject to fewer constraints on their methods of practice. The supply of resources available to low-income persons is thus inevitably interlocked with patterns of medical care for others.

One approach to national health insurance would limit population coverage to those who have made contributions to the social security system, on the assumption that people feel better if they believe, whether correctly or incorrectly, that they have "paid" for their benefits through systematic contributions. Thus, they are collectively more willing to submit to higher tax rates than they would be if the link between costs and benefits were not so direct. But excluding those outside the social security system would frequently exclude those who are most in need of assistance, thus undermining one of the basic goals of the plan.

One group that would be excluded if coverage were linked to the social security system consists of young adults who are no longer in school but have not yet found jobs. They would not be eligible for insurance under their parents' coverage, nor could they have their own policies. While this group is generally healthy, an accident or serious illness could result in burdensome medical bills that would inflict serious hardships on them or their parents.

Another approach to national health insurance would provide coverage under employer group plans, with separate plans for the poor, the aged, and those not eligible for coverage under an employer group plan. However, if few subsidies are provided for the latter group, the cost of coverage to them can be quite high. Under one such plan, a part-time worker earning $7,500 a year would have to pay an annual premium of $600. Self-employed workers, families with a disabled head, unemployed workers, or workers employed on a temporary or part-time basis would frequently be excluded from coverage because of the high cost of obtaining insurance without employer or government contributions. This would particularly affect families with incomes between about $5,000 and $10,000—those who are neither poor enough to qualify for governmental assistance nor sufficiently well to do to afford the full cost of the insurance.

An approach that provides coverage through employer groups can either require employers and employees to accept the plan or introduce some element of voluntarism. If employees may decline the plan, employers may exert some pressure on them to do so to minimize the cost to the employer. Compulsory coverage with substantial employer contributions, however, may place serious financial strains on employers who do not currently have good health insurance plans for workers.

Thus, while universal coverage does have disadvantages, the major goals of national health insurance cannot be achieved so long as there are segments of the population that do not have adequate protection against the high cost of medical care. Universal coverage without regard to family composition, employability, or social security contribution history seems to provide the most equitable solution.

What Should Be Covered?

Several considerations affect the choice of the range of medical services that should be covered under national health insurance. High priorities include: (1) medical services that reduce mortality or increase productivity, hence benefiting society as a whole; (2) medical services that can add substantially to the financial burden of medical care for an individual; (3) medical services that are so essential they will be sought regardless of the cost; (4) medical services that constitute acceptable lower-cost substitutes for covered services. The decision to include any given type of medical service in the benefit package, however, is separate from the decision to make the service available to all or a portion of covered persons free of any direct charge. Considerations bearing on that issue will be considered in the next section.

A number of medical services have been identified as having high social benefits because they reduce mortality or increase worker productivity. Prenatal care for women and immunizations and other basic care for babies are frequently cited. Mental health care, while its efficacy is somewhat more controversial, can have substantial benefits not only for those receiving care but for society as a whole through improved worker productivity, reduction in crime or antisocial behavior, and reduced dependence of the patient or family on public resources.

Items that can be quite costly include not only hospitalization and specialist physicians' fees but also lower-cost services that are required in great volume, such as weekly allergy shots, drugs for the proper management of chronic illness, and the periodic surveillance by a physician of conditions such as diabetes and hypertension. Some dental services and cosmetic surgery, despite their high cost, are typically excluded from coverage on the grounds that they are amenities that add to the enjoyment of life but are not essential to good health; as such they should be available only to those willing to pay for them, just as are sailboats, color television sets, and vacations abroad.

Since there is rarely only one possible treatment method for any given medical problem, it is important that choices be made among alternatives on the basis of the expected benefits in relation to cost. Covering only a limited range of services alters this calculation by reducing the net cost of some services to the patient but not others. For example, procedures may be carried out in a hospital that could be done in a hospital outpatient department or physician's office with recuperation at home. Nursing-home care for the elderly may come to be preferred over services rendered in the home by family or home health nurses. If prescription drugs are covered but not nonprescription drugs, more costly drugs may be used where others are equally efficacious. If insurance coverage is restricted to physician services, patients may not use less trained personnel for some services that can be adequately performed by them. Obviously, there must be a cut-off point for coverage, but it should be established on the basis of the degree of substitutability likely to occur, the cost savings of substitution, and the efficacy or quality of substitute forms of care.

There are some services that may be required for some groups of the population but not others. For example, residents of sparsely populated areas may need transportation assistance in order to receive needed medical services. Groups with lower levels of education may require "outreach" services to inform them of available care and of the importance of early medical intervention. These services might be more appropriately rendered by being offered to special groups through supplementary health programs.

Should Patients Share in Costs?

One of the more controversial issues in national health insurance is what role there should be for direct payments by patients. Plans commonly specify deductible amounts requiring the patient to pay all of the cost up to some figure and have coinsurance provisions requiring the patient to pay a fraction of all expenses above the deductible—the total called cost-sharing amounts. For example, a policy may require a family to pay (within the calendar year) all of the first $150 of medical expenses for each of three family members and then pay twenty-five cents of every additional dollar of medical expenses beyond that.

Cost-sharing provisions raise several important questions. Should all patients share in the cost of all services, or should some patients or services be exempt from cost sharing? If patient charges are included in a plan, how high should they be? Should they be the same for all patients regardless of income or financial resources? If the plan does not cover all expenses, should patients be permitted, or even encouraged, to purchase supplementary private insurance to cover the remainder?

Although lack of any cost sharing is increasingly recognized as inflationary and conducive to inefficient and wasteful use of resources, uniform cost-sharing provisions fall heavily upon the poor and substantial, unlimited cost sharing can cause heavy financial burdens for even the nonpoor.[1] One option would be to relate the amount of payments required of patients to their incomes and to set ceilings on how much any family would have to pay. While such a solution has obvious merit, it adds to the administrative complexity of the plan and requires the accumulation of sensitive data banks on income as well as health problems. Furthermore, little empirical evidence is available for judging the consequences of any given schedule of income-related cost-sharing requirements. This makes it important to preserve flexibility so that changes can be made in the plan over time as experience is gained.

Perhaps the best way to develop criteria to weigh the cost-sharing options is to review the basic goals of national health insurance. Clearly, substantial cost sharing by lower-income patients will deter them from seeking needed medical care and thus undermine the first major goal of national health insurance. An elderly couple struggling to make ends meet on social security payments of $3,000 a year cannot reasonably be expected to pay $150 for each deductible, 25 percent of the cost of additional hospital and medical bills, and all of the cost of excluded services such as eyeglasses, hearing aids, dentures, and prescription drugs. But an elderly couple with an income of $15,000 from a good retirement plan may be able to meet the cost-sharing amounts without undue burden. Thus, reducing or eliminating cost-sharing requirements for the lowest-income families is important in achieving the goals of national health insurance but is not necessary for all families.

It should be recognized that not all costs of medical care are direct ones. Use of medical services normally entails some time and transportation costs as well. These costs alone may be sufficient to curb any abuses of excessive care. Adding to these costs with even nominal cost-sharing amounts may deter use of needed medical services, particularly by the poor. Since the poor tend to live in areas with few medical resources, the time and travel costs required of them may be substantial. Furthermore,

1. See Karen Davis, "Lessons of Medicare and Medicaid for National Health Insurance," in National Health Insurance—Implications, Hearings before the Subcommittee on Public Health and Environment of the House Committee on Interstate and Foreign Commerce, 93 Cong. 1 sess., 2 sess. (1974), pp. 206–15 (Brookings Reprint 295).

the preference of many physicians for treating higher-income patients undoubtedly acts as a restraint on excessive use of services by the poor even without any direct monetary costs. It has sometimes been argued that making medical care free for everyone would give the poor an advantage since those who are willing to wait would eventually obtain the needed care and the cost of time to the poor is cheap. However, many working poor are unlikely to have generous sick leave provisions and so may lose income while obtaining medical care. Lower-income families are less likely to have an adult at home with time to seek out medical care for children. These indirect costs of medical care are sufficiently important for most poor people that adding direct monetary costs to their burden seems unjustified.

The second goal of national health insurance—preventing financial hardship for all families—clearly requires that a ceiling be placed on patient contributions, so that a family's payments will never exceed a fixed sum, such as $1,000, or a fixed percentage of income, such as 10 percent. If low-income families are not required to contribute toward their medical care, some mechanism for increasing the ceiling gradually as income rises must be devised. For example, families with incomes below $5,000 might not be required to pay any of their medical bills, families with incomes between $5,000 and $10,000 required to contribute up to 20 percent of their income in excess of $5,000, and families with incomes above $10,000 required to pay a maximum of $1,000. Thus, a family with a $5,000 income would pay nothing; a family with a $7,500 income would pay a maximum of $500; and a family with a $10,000 income or above would pay a maximum of $1,000.

Justification for Substantial Direct Patient Payments

While such sums may still seem sizable, there are strong justifications for retaining substantial direct payments by patients in a national health insurance plan. First, cost sharing reduces the cost of the plan, which must be financed through taxes or other sources. Plans that contain no deductible and coinsurance provisions would thus require massive increases in payroll and income taxes to finance expenditures that are currently made in the private sector. This would move into the federal budget private outlays for normal medical expenses that are now being made by middle- and upper-income groups with little financial strain. Furthermore, the large tax increases necessary to finance such a program might force the nation to give up other high-priority objectives. Experience with Medicare also suggests that even with adequate financing of medical care services budgetary funds would still be required for special programs to ensure access to medical care for minority groups and rural residents. Attempting to finance the entire cost of medical care through the federal budget, therefore, may impede other social programs as well as restrict budgetary outlays for medical care.

Second, cost sharing reduces (but does not eliminate) the need for administrative control over the use of medical services. Deductible and coinsurance amounts give patients and physicians an incentive to choose alternative forms of care: care on a less costly outpatient basis versus inpatient hospital care, care from family physicians rather than specialists, greater use of physician extenders and nurse practitioners for services not requiring a physician. In addition, it is important that the advantages of making additional units of medical care services available be weighed against the resources that must be devoted to providing them. While an extra day of hospital care, a follow-up visit to the physician, or an extra battery of laboratory tests may contribute to improved health, the resources required to provide these incremental services may have greater social value if diverted to other uses. Considerable evidence has accumulated that the presence or absence of cost-sharing provisions in insurance plans can have a substantial effect on the amount and mix of medical services.[2]

2. For evidence, see Anne A. Scitovsky and Nelda M. Snyder, "Effect of Coinsurance on Use of Physician Services," *Social Security Bulletin,* vol. 35 (June 1972), pp. 3–19; Charles E. Phelps and Joseph P. Newhouse, "Effect of Coinsurance: A Multivariate Analysis," ibid., pp. 20–28; Evelyn Peel and Jack Scharff, "Impact of Cost-Sharing on Use of Ambulatory Services under Medicare, 1969," *Social Security Bulletin,* vol. 36 (October 1973), pp. 3–24; Joseph P. Newhouse and Charles E. Phelps, *On Having Your Cake and Eating It Too: Econometric Problems in Estimating the Demand for Health Services,* R-1149-NC (Rand Corporation, 1974); Martin S. Feldstein, "Econometric Studies of Health Economics," Discussion Paper 291 (Harvard University, Harvard Institute of Economic Research, 1973; processed); Paul B. Ginsburg and Larry M. Manheim, "Insurance, Copayment, and Health Services Utilization: A Critical Review," *Journal of Economics and Business,* vol. 25 (Winter 1973), pp. 142–53; and Robert S. Kaplan and Lester B. Lave, "Patient Incentives and Hospital Insurance," *Health Services Research,* vol. 6 (Winter 1971), pp. 288–300. For studies indicating that patient payments have adverse effects on utilization of services by the poor, see Charles P. Hall, Jr., and others, "The Effects of Cost-Sharing in the Medicaid Program: Final Report" (Temple University, December 1973; processed); R. G. Beck, "The Effects of Co-Payment on the Poor," *Journal of Human Resources,* vol. 9 (Winter 1974), pp. 129–42; Merwyn R. Greenlick and others, "Comparing the Use of

In the absence of such financial incentives to weigh the cost of medical services to society, regulatory bodies must be established to review the necessity of hospitalization, the appropriateness of the length of hospital stay, and the efficacy of laboratory tests and ancillary services. Controls on the numbers of specialists, family physicians, other health personnel, and health facilities must be created and enforced. Unfortunately, the administrative expertise and accumulated knowledge required for such an undertaking is not yet available, nor is the question resolved of who should serve on such regulatory bodies.

In addition to providing important automatic incentives for the appropriate utilization of medical services, cost sharing can help reduce the charges that physicians and hospitals set for their services. This is especially important if the national health insurance plan contains no effective mechanism for placing a lid on reimbursement levels. For example, a physician who charges $5 to a patient without insurance may charge $20 when the patient pays only 25 percent of the bill, and substantially more when the patient pays none of the bill. Similarly, hospitals have increased charges as insurance coverage has grown, and hospital administrators have had no difficulty in finding ways to spend the increased revenues. Competition among health care providers, which admittedly works far from perfectly even in the absence of insurance, will not work at all without some direct patient payments, since patients have no reason to select a physician charging lower fees even if he or she provides exactly the same care with regard to convenience, quality, sensitivity, and all the other dimensions of this very personal service. Nor will either patient or physician have any incentive to select a lower-cost hospital, all other considerations being equal. In short, direct controls on costs are very difficult to enforce without providing some incentives for those who actually make the decisions.

These pressures for additional services and demands for higher reimbursement by providers could greatly increase the cost of medical services. A recent study by Newhouse and others estimates that absence of

---

Medical Care Services by a Medically Indigent and a General Membership Population in a Comprehensive Prepaid Group Practice Program." *Medical Care,* vol. 10 (May–June 1972), pp. 187–200. For dissenting points of view on the effect of patient payments, see C. Patrick Hardwick, Larry Shuman, and Shlomo Barnoon, "Effect of Participatory Insurance on Hospital Utilization," *Health Services Research,* vol. 7 (Spring 1972), pp. 43–57; and rejoinders to Kaplan and Lave (cited above), *Health Services Research* (Winter 1971).

any cost sharing would increase the demand for hospital inpatient services by approximately 5 to 15 percent (the low estimate reflects the already extensive third-party payment for hospital costs). Increased demand for ambulatory services would be much more dramatic—approximately 75 percent—since present coverage of such services is limited.[3]

Some increase in demand for services, particularly by lower-income people, is desirable; in fact, national health insurance would be a failure if it left existing patterns of medical care utilization unchanged. Increases in demand of this magnitude, however, may cause strains on the medical system. Newhouse notes that most of the increased demand for ambulatory services could not be fulfilled because of the limited supply of physicians and other providers. Inflationary pressures would build up, patients would experience longer delays in receiving appointments, and physicians might change the character of services provided (such as reducing time spent with each patient) and be more selective about the types of patients served.[4] Physicians might even decide to work fewer hours, since with rising fees they would be able to earn higher incomes from seeing fewer patients.

Feldstein and Friedman have attempted to estimate the increase in prices that would be induced by greater insurance coverage. They consider replacing current coverage with a plan that contains a deductible of $50 each for hospital care and medical services, a coinsurance rate of 20 percent, and a maximum ceiling on patient contributions of 10 percent of family income. Based upon studies of the way hospitals and physicians respond to insurance coverage, they estimate that this type of coverage would increase prices by 40 percent.[5] The inflationary impact of complete removal of patient payments would be even greater.

One way to resolve the dilemma of encouraging greater utilization of medical services by the poor without greatly increasing inflationary pressures would be to relate any cost-sharing provisions to income. Lower-income persons would have minimal or no direct costs, while others

3. Joseph P. Newhouse, Charles E. Phelps, and William B. Schwartz, "Policy Options and the Impact of National Health Insurance," *New England Journal of Medicine,* vol. 290 (June 13, 1974), pp. 1345–59.

4. Ibid.

5. Martin Feldstein and Bernard Friedman, "The Effect of National Health Insurance on the Price and Quantity of Medical Care," in Richard N. Rosett (ed.), *The Role of Health Insurance in the Health Services Sector,* A Conference of the Universities–National Bureau Committee for Economic Research (National Bureau of Economic Research, 1975).

Figure 4-1. Family Cost Sharing in National Health Insurance under an Illustrative Income-Related Plan[a]

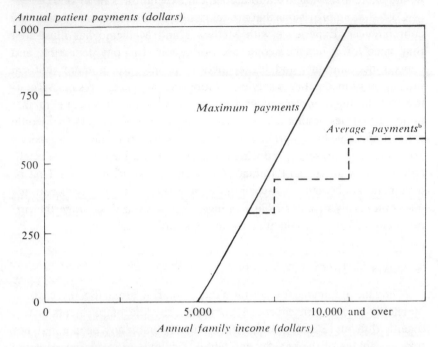

Annual patient payments (dollars)

Annual family income (dollars)

a. See text for description of the plan.
b. Based on a family of four with family member medical expenses of $550, $250, $150, and $50.

would be required to participate more fully in the cost of care. The following is illustrative of an income-related cost-sharing schedule. A family of four with an income below $5,000 would be excused from any direct payments. Families with incomes between $5,000 and $7,500 would be required to pay the first $50 of medical expenses for each of three family members and 20 percent of all expenses above that, with a ceiling on family payments set at 20 percent of income in excess of $5,000. Families with incomes between $7,500 and $10,000 would be required to pay the first $100 of medical expenses for each of three family members and 20 percent of all expenses above that, also with a ceiling of 20 percent of income in excess of $5,000. Finally, families with incomes above $10,000 would be required to pay the first $150 of medical expenses for each of three family members and 25 percent of all medical expenses above that, with a total ceiling of $1,000 on family contributions. Figure 4-1 illustrates the maximum family payments that would be required and average expenditures families at various income levels would make if they incurred total medical expenditures of $1,000.

Cost-sharing provisions that are related to income have other desirable consequences. Experience with Medicare and Medicaid has illustrated that when lower-income people are not required to pay deductible and coinsurance amounts and higher-income people are, a more uniform utilization of medical care services among income classes results.[6] Relating cost sharing to income in a systematic way should thus help eliminate major disparities among income classes in the use of services for people with comparable health problems. Income-related cost-sharing provisions are also a mechanism for reducing the adverse work incentives that might be created by an abrupt termination of benefits as income rises. That is, termination of benefits at, say, a family income of $5,000, may discourage a second family member from seeking a job or even discourage the primary earner from moonlighting or undertaking overtime work.

Limitations of Cost-Sharing Provisions

While the arguments for substantial cost sharing are many, there would inevitably be some ill effects. A complex schedule of payments is frequently difficult to understand, with the result that many people may not take advantage of the benefits available. This danger is minimized if the plan assumes responsibility for paying providers and billing patients for their share.

If cost sharing is related to income, some administrative mechanism must be devised for obtaining income information in a way that protects the individual from as much infringement of privacy as possible. One alternative would be for the Internal Revenue Service to issue a health "credit card" coded with the appropriate income information. Patients would charge services to the card and the administering agency would then pay the medical care provider and bill the patient for his or her share of the bill.

Imposition of cost-sharing amounts may also discourage some needed medical care, deter patients from seeking early treatment for a serious

6. Karen Davis and Roger Reynolds, "The Impact of Medicare and Medicaid on Access to Medical Care," in Rosett (ed.), *The Role of Health Insurance in the Health Services Sector.*

symptom, or cause patients to forgo beneficial preventive care. Preventive services of proven efficacy, however, can be exempted from deductible amounts if payment for such services can be shown to deter even high-income people from seeking this form of care.

The merits of cost-sharing provisions may be eroded in two ways: first, many people may purchase supplementary private insurance to pick up the deductible and coinsurance amounts; second, the importance of fixed cost-sharing amounts may be reduced over time by inflation in medical care costs. Under national health insurance there is no rationale for subsidizing the purchase of supplementary insurance. Any contributions by an employer to supplementary insurance should be counted as taxable income to the employee and not as a legitimate business expense of the firm. Deductions for health insurance and medical expenses under the personal income tax should also be eliminated. The real value of cost-sharing amounts can be retained by escalator clauses that automatically adjust deductible and maximum liability amounts to changes over time in average health expenditures per capita.

Unfortunately, the complete ramifications of cost sharing are not well known. Very little is known about how the use of supplementary private insurance would vary with different income-related cost-sharing schedules; even less is known about how such schedules would affect the mix of essential and marginal care. A national health insurance experiment was recently initiated by the U.S. Department of Health, Education, and Welfare to find answers to some of these questions, but even preliminary results will not be available for a couple of years.[7] In the meantime, experience with Medicare emphatically suggests that uniform cost-sharing provisions will lead to wide disparities in utilization among income classes but that reduced cost sharing for lower-income people can allow them to adopt patterns of medical care utilization similar to those of middle- and upper-income persons with similar health problems.[8] Given the unknown consequences of either including or omitting cost sharing, retention of cost sharing, with the flexibility to alter schedules over time as experience is gained, seems to be the best approach.

7. For a description of the experiment, see Joseph P. Newhouse, "A Design for a Health Insurance Experiment," *Inquiry,* vol. 11 (March 1974), pp. 5–27.

8. See Davis and Reynolds, "The Impact of Medicare and Medicaid on Access to Medical Care," and Peel and Scharff, "Impact of Cost-sharing on Use of Ambulatory Services Under Medicare, 1969."

How Should the Plan Be Financed?

A decision about the appropriate method or methods of financing health insurance must weigh a number of objectives: (1) avoiding a regressive tax structure; (2) preventing adverse effects on employment; and (3) minimizing any windfall gains to those currently financing medical care. These objectives, however, are not absolute and may be altered by the mix of financing for other public goods and services.

Equity in Financing

A method of financing is considered to be regressive if its cost represents a higher fraction of income for lower-income than for higher-income families. In the case of national health insurance, the cost is the sum of premiums and taxes (whether payroll or other federal and state taxes) paid by the family, either directly or indirectly.

The distribution of insurance benefits by income classes under the plan may influence the degree of progressivity or regressivity deemed appropriate.[9] Differences in benefits among income classes may arise either because family composition varies by income class (for example, many low-income families are one- or two-person elderly families) or because the benefits of the plan vary directly with income. The plan may require lower cost sharing by lower-income families, thus diverting a larger than proportionate share of benefits to the poor. The poor may also receive more benefits because of their greater incidence of medical problems. The actual distribution of benefits, however, will also depend on variations in total medical expenditures by income class. That is, cost-sharing provisions are less of a deterrent to the use of medical services by higher-income families, and medical resources are more readily available to them. Therefore, higher-income families may have greater total medical expenditures, which offsets somewhat the lower proportion of the total bill paid by the insurance plan. In comparing the progressivity or regressivity of two plans that differ in their distribution of benefits as well as costs, it is useful to examine the distribution of *net benefits*—that is,

9. This point has been made by Martin Feldstein, Bernard Friedman, and Harold Luft in "Distributional Aspects of National Health Insurance Benefits and Finance," *National Tax Journal,* vol. 25 (December 1972), pp. 497–510. Many of the concepts discussed in this section are explored in greater detail there.

insurance benefits less premiums or taxes paid into the plan—among income classes.

Another measure of the distributional effects of a national health insurance plan would have to include medical expenditures not covered by the plan. If lower-income families are not required to make any direct payments while higher-income families must pay most of their medical expenses directly, the cost of medical care will fall more heavily on higher-income families. The average total payment, including direct patient payments as well as premiums and taxes paid, indicates the complete cost of medical care to the family. If the total level of medical care varies by income, this measure of cost does not apply to a constant amount of medical care. Thus, some families with a higher average total payment may obtain more medical care for their contribution than a family with lower average total payment.

Financing for most national health insurance plans is based upon premiums, payroll tax revenues, and federal and state general revenues. Financing by premiums paid directly by employers or private individuals to private insurance companies has the effect of limiting the federal budgetary cost of the plan. If the premium is mandatory, however, this lower budgetary cost is largely illusory because the compulsory premium contribution is actually no different from a tax assessed on the employer for purposes of providing the benefits. In fact, if a firm responds to this premium by lowering cash wages or raising them less than it would otherwise, the premium is borne by the employee. In this case, it becomes a regressive tax, representing a much higher share of income for low-income groups. For example, if the total premium cost were $600, workers with incomes of $15,000 would pay 4 percent of their incomes for the premium while workers with incomes of $6,000 would pay 10 percent of their incomes.

The payroll tax, while not a progressive source of financing like the income tax, is markedly less regressive than a fixed premium per family. For example, if the insurance plan were financed by a 4 percent tax on the first $20,000 of family earnings, all families earning below $20,000 would pay a constant 4 percent rather than the higher percentage that low-income workers would pay with a fixed premium. Reform of the payroll tax could further mitigate its regressive nature. One step in this direction would be to make the tax applicable to all earnings. Its burden on two-worker and low-income families could be further lightened by providing rebates or subsidies to low-income workers. If the payroll tax were combined with a tax on unearned income (dividends, interest, rent, capital gains, transfer payments, and so forth), the overall tax burden could be made more proportional to total income. Heavy reliance on the progressive personal income tax as a method of financing would make such reform less urgent.

The cost of health insurance should not only be fairly borne by families of varying incomes, but families with the same income should be treated equally. Making all sources of income subject to taxes is one means of achieving this end. Special difficulties arise, however, in plans that rely on premiums as a method of financing. Policies sold by private health insurance companies typically have higher premiums for small groups, the self-employed, and groups that include some poor health risks. Thus, a family may find that its cost is higher because of the type of employment or nature of the group to which it belongs even though it receives the same benefits as another family with the same income. Even when payroll or general taxes are used, a family living in an area with limited medical resources and low medical prices may receive lower payments from the plan than a family with the same income and premiums that lives in an area with ample medical resources of high quality and specialization.

Employment Effects

The way in which national health insurance is financed can also have important effects on the demand and supply of labor. An employer may be unable to shift the cost of a premium to workers if wages are already at the minimum wage level. For these low-wage employers, the premium is much the same as an increase in the minimum wage, thus raising the cost of workers to the firm. If the increase in cost is substantial, some low-wage employers may either go out of business or substantially reduce their labor force.[10] Employers would also have a strong incentive to hire

10. An excellent discussion of the adverse economic effects of premiums is contained in a criticism by the Department of Health, Education, and Welfare of the administration's original national health insurance proposal:

"Employer mandated health insurance coverage would have the following economic effects:

1. The income distribution consequences would be regressive with regard to both the financing and to a lesser extent, the benefit structure. NHISA [the former administration plan] would be financed by a fixed tax per employee that is unrelated to

part-time workers, secondary family earners, or those who decline the insurance.

In addition to influencing employer preferences among employees or the employment opportunities offered to different types of workers, a health insurance plan may affect people's willingness to work by imposing high marginal tax rates on additional earnings. Marginal tax rates on income net of medical expenses are affected by a reduction in benefits and an increase in costs as income rises.[11] In some plans, reduction in benefits and increases in costs may more than offset additional earnings, so that the marginal tax rate exceeds 100 percent. A working family that finds itself with less money to spend on nonmedical expenses after a pay raise, after working overtime, or after a second earner enters the labor force may feel resentful and reluctant to work as hard.

Windfall Gains

Finally, the choice of methods of financing should depend to some extent on current sources of payment. In 1975, it is estimated that employers will contribute $20 billion to employee health insurance plans, and state and local governments will contribute $6.3 billion to public health insurance plans.[12] If no consideration were given to these payments, employers and state governments would gain from the plan. If the

---

earnings. Thus, the proportion of earnings that would be devoted to NHISA premiums would be greatest among low income workers. . . .
2. The economic effect on the labor market of mandated coverage is identical to that of an increase in the minimum wage of an amount equivalent to the employer's share of premiums. . . . The dislocation occurs for those marginal workers who are at the minimum wage. A strong equity argument can be made that, if the Federal government wishes to mandate coverage, it ought to help pay for it.
3. Since small employers as a group offer their employees less generous health insurance benefits than large employers, they would be most affected by the requirement to offer a minimum benefit package."

Caspar W. Weinberger to be Secretary of Health, Education, and Welfare, Hearings before the Senate Committee on Labor and Public Welfare, 93 Cong. 1 sess. (1973), pt. 2, p. 21a.

11. If the family is more concerned with premiums and taxes and not as aware of reductions in medical benefits as income rises, the marginal gross tax rate—defined as the increase in costs as income rises—may be a more appropriate measure of work disincentive.

12. U.S. Department of Health, Education, and Welfare, *Estimated Health Expenditures under Selected National Health Insurance Bills,* A Report to the Congress (1974), p. 3.

balance between federal and state government expenditures is desirable, a continuing contribution from the states may be in order. While reductions in contributions by employers to health insurance plans might eventually result in higher wages, some windfall gains to employers may occur if they are relieved of responsibility for currently scheduled payments. To avoid such gains, employers could be required to contribute to premiums or payroll taxes at least the amount they currently pay under private health insurance plans. Gradual reductions could be implemented over time if continuing employer contributions were not required.

What Role Should Private Insurance Companies and State Governments Have?

A wide range of administrative arrangements in a national health insurance plan is possible. Private health insurance companies could be charged with selling plans, underwriting coverage, and making profits. Alternatively, their role could be limited to that of administrative agents of a public plan, simply processing claims and making payments but not setting premiums and underwriting coverage. Or they could be totally replaced by a publicly administered plan. Similarly, state governments could be charged with regulating health insurance companies, establishing methods of paying medical care providers, and guaranteeing quality standards, either with or without general federal guidelines, or the federal government could assume all of these roles. States could participate in the subsidy of medical care for low-income persons, or all costs could be assumed federally.

Private Health Insurance Industry

The private health insurance industry has grown from an infant industry in 1940 to one with an estimated sales volume of $32.5 billion in 1975.[13] Insurance companies, acting as administrative agents for the Medicare program, will also cover another $13 billion of medical care expenditures in 1975. In addition, several states contract with private insurance companies for the administration of Medicaid claims. Any national health insurance plan that does not have a role for private companies could result in substantial displacement effects.

13. Department of Health, Education, and Welfare, *Estimated Health Expenditures Under Selected National Health Insurance Bills,* p. 3.

Administrative expenses under the Medicare and Medicaid programs have been considerably lower than for private health insurance plans, averaging 5 percent of benefit expenses in recent years. A valid comparison with private plans is difficult, however, because of the population covered. For one thing, the elderly tend to have larger average claims, so the administrative cost per dollar of benefits is low. Medicaid covers a population with greater than average health problems, so the average claim size may be greater there as well. Government plans may not capture all types of costs included in private plans, particularly capital costs, but they also provide additional services to the community such as ensuring quality and safety standards and enforcing discrimination provisions. The health insurance industry points to the experience of several large groups—such as the privately run federal employees indemnity benefit plan, where operating expenses are 3 percent of benefits, and other large groups that cover 50,000 or more employees, where expenses average 2.9 percent of benefits—to suggest that private plans could have much lower administrative costs if the size of their groups were comparable to those of the Medicare and Medicaid programs.[14] A recent study by the Department of Health, Education, and Welfare, however, shows that administrative expenses of the Medicaid program have been 30 percent higher in states that contract with private insurance companies for administration rather than administering the program directly.[15]

The performance of private health insurance companies has been varied and difficult to assess. For the most part, the industry has had great difficulty in staying ahead of rapidly rising medical prices, so that profits do not appear to be high. During the period of price controls beginning in late 1971, private health insurance companies appear to have experienced more rapid increases in premium income than in claims expenses.[16] However, since private insurance companies are not required to report income from investment of reserves, no measure of overall profitability of the industry is available. As shown in Table 4-1, Blue Cross–Blue Shield plans averaged a net income of 4.0 percent of premium income in 1972. Claims and operating expenses of other insurance com-

14. Testimony of Frederick E. Rathgeber, in *National Health Insurance,* Hearings before the House Committee on Ways and Means, 93 Cong. 2 sess. (1974), vol. 4, p. 1528.

15. HEW, Touche Ross Study of State Agency and Fiscal Agent Performance under Medicaid (unpublished; ca. 1973).

16. Marjorie S. Mueller, "Private Health Insurance in 1972: Health Care Services, Enrollment, and Finances," *Social Security Bulletin,* vol. 37 (February 1974), p. 32.

Table 4-1. Financial Experience of Private Health Insurance Organizations, 1972
Millions of dollars

						Net income	
Type of plan	Total income	Subscription or premium income	Claims expense	Operating expense	Net underwriting gain	Amount	As percent of premium income
Blue Cross–Blue Shield	10,079	9,923	8,991	689	243	399	4.0
Blue Cross	7,175	7,067	6,501	365	201	309	4.4
Blue Shield	2,904	2,856	2,490	324	43	90	3.2
Insurance companies	n.a.	10,905	9,120	2,334	−548	n.a.	n.a.
Group policies	n.a.	8,309	7,754	1,113	−558	n.a.	n.a.
Individual policies	n.a.	2,596	1,366	1,220	10	n.a.	n.a.
Independent[a]	1,517	1,499	1,381	112	5	24	1.6
All plans	n.a.	22,327	19,492	3,135	−300	n.a.	n.a.

Source: Marjorie S. Mueller, "Private Health Insurance in 1972: Health Care Services, Enrollment, and Finances," *Social Security Bulletin*, vol. 37 (February 1974), table 13, p. 32. Figures are rounded.
n.a. Not available.
a. These include community, employer-employee-union, private group clinic, and dental service corporation plans.

panies exceeded premium income in 1972, but these losses may have been made up by income on investments.

The cost of insurance, measured as the difference between premium payments and benefit expenditures, has varied from plan to plan. Table 4-2 shows that in 1972 operating expenses as a percent of premium income averaged 5.2 percent in Blue Cross plans, 11.3 percent in Blue Shield plans, 13.4 percent in other group plans, and 47.0 percent in other individual insurance plans. This measure of cost, however, is sensitive to the size and frequency of claims and the mix of services insured. Differences in operating expenses per enrollee are not so marked, averaging $5 per enrollee in both Blue Cross and Blue Shield plans, $13 in other group plans, and $24 in other individual plans. Low operating expenses, however, may result in excessive benefit expenses if claims are not carefully reviewed. Thus low operating expenses do not necessarily imply efficient operation.

In spite of the conflicting evidence about the relative efficiency of public and private insurance administration, it is clear that over a billion dollars of marketing costs could be saved by federal administration of a national health insurance plan. Complete elimination of the industry, however, would cause substantial dislocation, and an intermediate role as administrative agent seems justified. Competitive bidding for this role

Table 4-2. Operating Expenses and Retentions of Private Health Insurance
Organizations, 1972

Type of plan	Operating expense as percent of premium income	Operating expenses per enrollee (dollars)	Retentions as percent of premium income
Blue Cross	5.2	5.05	8.0
Blue Shield	11.3	5.07	12.8
Insurance companies			
Group policies	13.4	13.05	6.7
Individual policies	47.0	24.45	47.4
Independent[a]	7.5	9.77	7.8
All plans	14.0	...	12.7

Source: Same as Table 4-1, pp. 32, 37, 38.
a. See Table 4-1, note a, for definition.

should help to weed out the most inefficient carriers. Reform of the industry to make it more responsive to consumers and less responsive to the wishes of medical care providers should also help to curb some of the abuses that have occurred in the Blue Cross–Blue Shield plans.[17]

State Governments

The major roles that have been proposed for state governments in national health insurance are to regulate the private insurance industry, establish standards for participation and payment methods and levels for medical care providers, and administer and subsidize coverage for low-income families.

Combining some of these roles can create dilemmas for state governments. For example, if a state is charged with establishing fee levels for physicians, it must trade off pressures to set higher fees that would attract physicians to the state against the lower fees that would minimize the cost of the low-income plan. If experience with Medicaid is any guide, those states with the most limited medical resources would also have the least attractive physician reimbursement levels, while the states that could afford to heavily subsidize care for the poor are likely to have the most generous reimbursement levels, even though they are also likely to have the least need for additional health manpower.

17. See Sylvia A. Law, *Blue Cross: What Went Wrong?* (Yale University Press, 1974).

Since newly trained medical manpower is largely mobile from state to state, a federal reimbursement policy would seem to be indicated. Experimentation with other roles for state governments, with appropriate federal guidelines, might also be a worthwhile undertaking.

What Role Should Consumers Have?

An often forgotten component of a national health insurance plan is a clearly defined role for consumers. Although consumers have frequently had little say in the formulation and operation of a plan, their participation on a number of levels should help to ensure that the system is flexible and responsive to the needs of those it is designed to serve.[18]

First, it is important that grievance processes be established so that consumers may channel complaints quickly and efficiently and without substantial legal expenses. Periodic hearings should also be held to uncover deficiencies in the coverage or operation of the plan. Second, consumers should be guaranteed representation on all important policy-setting or advisory boards. Preferably, these positions would be elected ones, thus minimizing the danger that the so-called public members are really appointed by those with vested interests in the plan. Finally, safeguards for patient privacy are essential in any plan collecting massive amounts of sensitive medical information. Patients should have a right to examine their own records, and patient approval of the release of any medical information should be required. If the plan requires income information, this should be obtained in a manner that does not reveal personal income to medical care providers, other patients, or private companies.

How Should Hospitals, Physicians, and Other Providers Be Paid?

One of the most difficult issues to resolve in a national health insurance plan is how to pay providers of services. Since cooperation of hospitals, physicians, and other providers is essential to the success of the plan, any

18. For a discussion of the emerging role of consumers in health care organizations, see Cecil G. Sheps, "The Influence of Consumer Sponsorship on Medical Services," *Milbank Memorial Fund Quarterly*, vol. 50, no. 4, pt. 2 (October 1972), pp. 41–69.

substantial reduction in their relative incomes or change in their modes of practice may thwart the objectives of the plan. Yet one important objective of national health insurance is to limit rises in medical costs and encourage more efficient use of resources. Solutions to this dilemma are not easily found.

The first issue is whether reimbursement or payment by the insurance plan should constitute total payment for services, or whether physicians, hospitals, and others should be permitted to charge some patients, or all patients, more than the plan allows.

The Medicare program has permitted physicians to determine on each claim whether or not to accept assignment—that is, to accept the allowed charge as payment in full. On approximately 57 percent of the claims, physicians do accept assignment, but this fraction has been declining in recent years as Medicare has sought to tighten the level of reimbursement. In fiscal 1973, the difference between billed and allowed charges on unassigned claims under Medicare amounted to $214.3 million. This amount represents one-eighth of aggregate private expenditures by the aged for physicians' services.[19] Thus, experience with Medicare suggests that if given an option many physicians may choose to charge more than the allowed reimbursement, thus undermining the objectives of the plan, which are to ensure that medical care is not unduly expensive for those with limited means, to eliminate the financial burden of medical care for all, and to restrain cost increases.

More physicians may choose to accept assignment if they must select one fee basis for all patients, if they are relieved of bad debts and billing costs, and if they are offered other inducements such as free malpractice insurance.[20] However, under any plan that greatly increases inflationary pressures—and one study has estimated that demand for ambulatory services would increase by 75 percent under a full-coverage plan[21]—many physicians would be tempted to set fees at more than the allowed charge. Requiring physicians to accept assignment for certain classes of patients, such as the poor and elderly, so as to protect those who cannot pay from the financial consequences of nonassignment, may well simply reduce the

19. Testimony of Caspar W. Weinberger, in *National Health Insurance*, Hearings, vol. 2, pp. 601–02.

20. Free malpractice insurance was proposed by Wilbur J. Cohen in testimony before the House Committee on Ways and Means in June 1974. See *National Health Insurance*, vol. 7, p. 2762.

21. Newhouse and others, "Policy Options and the Impact of National Health Insurance," p. 1346.

supply of physician services available to them. Physicians, finding that they can earn higher incomes from other patients, may refuse to take patients for whom assignment is required or may give them lower-quality care. Such practices could reinforce the tradition of two-class medicine that national health insurance should help to eliminate.

Even if the physician is required to accept the reimbursement level established by the plan as allowable, several choices among reimbursement methods may be made. Physicians could be reimbursed on the basis of customary or usual fees according to a preestablished fee schedule, on a salary basis, or on a capitation basis. Each method of reimbursement has its own set of incentives, and abuses can occur under any method. Physicians paid on a fee basis may increase the number of services provided, such as by repeat office visits or additional tests and procedures, in order to increase their incomes. Physicians paid on a salary or capitation basis may try to restrict the number of services provided and the time spent with each patient in order to increase leisure time. Usual and customary fee reimbursement probably has the greatest inflationary potential, and it preserves the incentives now operative for the distribution of medical personnel. A uniform national payment plan, on the other hand, would provide positive incentives for physicians to locate in lower-cost areas, which are frequently areas with a shortage of medical services, rather than in areas with a surplus of services where demand from high-income patients has led to high monetary rewards for physicians. Fee schedules, if developed by the medical profession, may reward those with the greatest power in the profession, such as specialists and physicians affiliated with medical schools, and penalize physicians engaging in primary care or family practice.

There are also a number of methods possible for reimbursement of institutional providers. Reimbursement methods that would determine payment in advance of the provision of services, and independently of cost experiences, have been suggested. However, experience with such methods in Canada has shown them to be largely ineffective in containing costs.[22] Other proposals would gear reimbursement to the level of all hospitals of a given type in a given geographical area, rather than to the actual cost experience of the individual hospital. Still others would devise formulas taking into account the diagnostic mix of patients served, the

22. Robert G. Evans, "Beyond the Medical Marketplace: Expenditure, Utilization and Pricing of Insured Health Care in Canada," in Rosett (ed.), *The Role of Health Insurance in the Health Services Sector.*

level of services provided, and adjustment for quality differences.[23] Unfortunately, only limited experience has been obtained under any of these methods, and little is known about the efficacy of any one procedure. Experiments currently being conducted by the Social Security Administration and others should make possible more informed judgments about appropriate institutional reimbursement methods.

How Should the Plan Change Over Time?

Since answers to all the basic questions about the most appropriate form of national health insurance cannot be formulated before enactment of a plan, it is important that any plan adopted be flexible enough that it can be altered as experience is gained. Mechanisms for collecting appropriate data on performance and for feeding this information back into improved design are important features to be included in any plan.

It can be anticipated, however, that several features of the plan will require automatic adjustment over time—namely, those that are sensitive to overall changes in prices and incomes in the economy. Thus, it makes sense to build in automatic escalator clauses initially. Deductible amounts, for example, should be adjusted upward over time at the same rate as the average level of expenditures on medical services in order to preserve the original cost-sharing relationships. Income classes should also be adjusted upward as money incomes rise over time. Reimbursement of providers should likewise be tied to experience. Rather than tying physician *fees* to an appropriate economic index, tying *average physician expenditures* under the plan to an index would prevent physicians from increasing incomes by proliferating services.

23. Judith R. Lave, Lester B. Lave, and Lester P. Silverman, "A Proposal for Incentive Reimbursement for Hospitals," *Medical Care*, vol. 11 (March–April 1973), pp. 79–90.

chapter five **Alternative National Health Insurance Proposals**

Several national health insurance plans have been proposed in the past few years.[1] Some, such as the proposal originally backed by the American Medical Association, would rely on tax credits to induce greater coverage under private health insurance plans. Another proposal, sponsored by Senators Russell B. Long and Abraham A. Ribicoff, would replace Medicaid with a federal plan for the poor and cover catastrophic expenses for everyone. The administration, the American Hospital Association, and the Health Insurance Association of America have all backed bills that would rely heavily on basic and catastrophic health insurance by private insurance companies, with government contributions for care of the poor. Proposals that rely more heavily on public insurance include the compromise plan proferred by Senator Edward M. Kennedy and Congressman Wilbur D. Mills in 1974. The Health Security Act, originally introduced by Senator Kennedy and Congresswoman Martha W. Griffiths and still backed by the AFL-CIO, would replace private insurance with a federal program covering virtually all medical bills for U.S. residents. The following discussion shows how each of these proposals resolves the basic issues discussed in Chapter 4. While modifications in these plans can be expected and new plans will undoubtedly be introduced, these proposals represent the major alternatives under serious consideration in Congress.

1. For a more complete description of bills discussed in this chapter and other national health insurance proposals, see Saul Waldman, *National Health Insurance Proposals: Provisions of Bills Introduced in the 93rd Congress as of July 1974,* U.S. Social Security Administration, Office of Research and Statistics, DHEW Publication (SSA) 75-11920 (1974), and ibid., *as of February 1975.*

Tax Credit Approach

The medicredit proposal, originally sponsored by the American Medical Association and introduced by Representatives Richard H. Fulton and Joel T. Broyhill, would offer income tax credits for individuals purchasing a qualified private health insurance plan.[2]

Medicredit

Coverage under the plan would be voluntary and open to any individual under the age of 65. Medicare would be retained for the elderly without change, and the Medicaid program would continue on a more limited basis, paying any share of payments required of low-income patients under the qualified health plan and providing services not covered under the plan, such as drugs and most nursing-home care.

The amount of credit against federal income taxes would be equal to the full premium cost of the catastrophic component of the insurance. An additional credit would be allowed for the premium cost of the basic benefits; the full credit would be given to families with no tax liability and would be gradually scaled downward to 10 percent of the premium for families with tax liabilities of $891 or more, which corresponds on average to an adjusted gross income of about $10,000 or higher. Families with insufficient liability against which to offset the credit would receive a voucher equal to the difference for use in buying insurance.

Current tax deductions for direct medical expenses would be replaced by the tax credit. Employers could deduct the full cost of contributions to a qualified plan as business expenses; in addition, employees could count 80 percent of the employer's contribution to a qualified plan as if it were his or her own contribution.

The basic plan would provide sixty days a year of hospital care, subject to a $50 deductible per stay. Two days of care in a skilled nursing facility could be substituted for each day of covered hospital care, with a $50 deductible for each stay. Other services would generally be subject to a 20 percent coinsurance but with a maximum annual limit of $100 per family for physician, laboratory, and X-ray services combined, a separate $100 limit for hospital outpatient and home health services, and a separate limit

2. The AMA withdrew its support of this bill in 1975; but a tax credit approach still appeals to some members of Congress.

of $100 for dental care. Drugs, preventive services, and family planning services (unless provided by a physician) would not be covered.

The catastrophic plan would cover unlimited hospital care, after the family has incurred out-of-pocket payments on all medical services in excess of 10 percent of income. Some additional nursing-home care would also be provided by the catastrophic plan.

Although the insurance is voluntary, the prescribed plan for which the credit would be available is more liberal than most existing plans, and presumably most people now holding private insurance would switch to the new plan because of the considerable tax savings they would enjoy. The U.S. Department of Health, Education, and Welfare estimates that only 4 million Americans would not be covered by the plan, and most of those would probably have some other insurance, though perhaps more limited than the qualified plan.[3]

The plan would specifically prohibit federal supervision of medical fees or any control over the practice of medicine or the manner in which services are provided. Private insurance companies would be required to pay providers of medical services according to their customary charges. A national health insurance advisory board, at least five of whose eleven members would be required to be physicians, would establish administrative regulations and issue federal standards to the state insurance departments charged with certifying carriers and policies as qualified.

Disadvantages of the Medicredit Approach

The primary problem with this plan is the absence of any real incentive to curb inflation in the costs of medical care or to induce efficiency in the use of medical resources. Although the basic plan incorporates some deductible and coinsurance provisions, these are not structured in a way that would give them substantial influence on individual decisions. Hospital cost sharing would consist of a fixed deductible for each stay and would not depend on the length of stay or the costliness of the hospital selected. The maximum that any family would have to pay for physician, laboratory, and X-ray services combined would be $100 annually. It is unlikely that this maximum would cause middle- and upper-income families to weigh the benefits of alternative medical resources against their costs or to

3. Estimates of population coverage for all plans discussed in this chapter are from U.S. Department of Health, Education, and Welfare, *Estimated Health Expenditures under Selected National Health Insurance Bills,* A Report to the Congress (1974).

go to physicians who charge less. The only significant constraints on hospital use would apply to stays beyond sixty days, and it is those stays that are least likely to be elective. Only the very poor would find the nominal cost-sharing payments a deterrent to the use of needed medical services, and these amounts would be paid by Medicaid for the recipients of public assistance.

The plan also has some flaws caused by its link to the tax system. The tax subsidies would result automatically in forgone tax revenues that would not be subject to congressional approval. Furthermore, the amount of the subsidy would be somewhat arbitrary, since it would depend on the amount of a family's tax liability, which is sensitive to all the loopholes in the tax laws. For example, homeowners, who can deduct interest and property taxes, have lower tax liabilities and would receive greater medical insurance subsidies than would renters.

Indirect payment of medical care through a tax subsidy also eliminates the possibility of using the financing of medical care to place restrictions on the cost or quality of care.

Finally, the plan would leave the Medicare program unchanged, providing no remedies for its inadequate catastrophic coverage, its failure to provide coverage for all of the elderly, and its deterrent effect on the use of medical services by the low-income elderly not on Medicaid.

Alternative Types of Tax Credits—The Brock Proposal

Many of the flaws of the medicredit proposal are not intrinsic to the tax credit approach but result from the limited cost sharing under the plans, the provisions restricting federal control or supervision of costs and quality, the reliance on private health insurance policies, and the limited coverage. Tax credits for medical expenses could be designed to avoid many of these deficiencies.

One such proposal has been recently introduced by Senator William E. Brock III. His Medical Expense Tax Credit Act would provide a tax credit not for health insurance premiums but for direct medical expenses. All Americans would be eligible for a tax credit for any direct medical expenses in excess of 15 percent of modified adjusted gross income (that is, adjusted gross income, as defined by the Internal Revenue Service, less personal exemptions, currently $750 per person). The tax credit would apply to 85 percent of all medical expenses in excess of the income limit. It would be a part of the personal income tax return, and people with tax liabilities less than the amount of the credit would receive a refund.

To illustrate how the plan would work, consider a family of four with a $9,000 income and health care expenses of $2,000.[4] Modified Internal Revenue Service adjusted gross income would be $6,000—$9,000 less four times $750. The tax credit would then be computed as follows:

Eligible medical expenses	$2,000
Less 15 percent of modified	
adjusted gross income	900
Difference	1,100
Tax credit or refund (85	
percent of difference)	935

Such an approach has many advantages. It is simple to understand, easy to administer, and mitigates the financial hardship of very high medical expenses for most middle- and upper-income families. Medicaid would be continued in order to provide financial access to medical care for those on welfare. However, many low-income families not eligible for Medicaid would find outlays of 15 percent of income for medical care prohibitive. Many of the poor, therefore, would still not have access to needed medical services. Reducing the income deductible for low-income groups to, say, 3 or 5 percent of income would greatly assist the poor. Providing for loans against the credit would help relieve the hardship incurred from a delay in reimbursement until the end of the tax year. A deductible of 15 percent of income, plus unlimited coinsurance of 15 percent on expenses above the income deductible, could also be a financial burden for many working-class families. Reducing the income deductible to 8 or 10 percent of income and setting a maximum limit on family contributions of, say, $1,500 or $2,000 for all families above the median income level would improve the protection afforded by the plan. These changes could easily be written into the tax code, without increasing the complexity of administration.

The major disadvantage of the tax credit approach is that it does not tie payment of medical services to control over the cost or quality of services provided. Supplementary cost and quality controls would be an essential part of reliance on subsidies through the tax system. This proposal would also do little to change the structure of private health insurance coverage. While it would assist those with inadequate catastrophic protection and those considered poor health risks who are unable to obtain health insurance coverage, the excessive coverage of short hospital stays under private health insurance plans is likely to persist.

4. William E. Brock III, *Congressional Record,* daily ed., June 19, 1974, p. S10868.

Table 5-1. Estimated Tax Subsidies for Medical Expenses under Current Law and Alternative Proposals, by Income Class, 1974[a]

Adjusted gross income class (dollars)	Current law	Proposal I[b]	Proposal 2[c]
	Millions of dollars		
All classes	2,625	2,227	3,399
	Percentage distribution		
Under 5,000	2.1	27.4	23.4
5,000–9,999	18.7	43.3	43.2
10,000–14,999	21.6	9.7	13.1
15,000 and over	57.7	19.4	20.3
Total	100.0	100.0	100.0

Source: Derived from the Brookings file of 1970 individual income tax returns, with data projected to calendar year 1974 levels. Percentages are rounded.

a. Neither proposal includes the $3 billion tax subsidy in 1974 attributable to the exclusion of employer contributions to health insurance plans from taxable personal income. Estimates are based on the tax returns of those who currently itemize medical deductions. Many with low incomes who do not now itemize deductions would be eligible for benefits under a tax credit plan. Tax subsidies shown, therefore, are underestimated. The estimates do not consider any changes in prices, use of medical services, or health insurance coverage induced by the credit.

b. Full tax credit for all health insurance and medical expenses in excess of 15 percent of income, with credit in excess of tax refundable.

c. Full tax credit for all health insurance and medical expenses in excess of 10 percent of income, with credit in excess of tax refundable.

Since the proposal would replace existing personal income tax deductions for health insurance and medical expenses, it could be achieved at little or no additional cost. Table 5-1 indicates the distributional effects of replacing these current deductions by a full tax credit for all medical expenses in excess of 15 percent and 10 percent of income.

Poor and Catastrophic Coverage Approach

Another approach to national health insurance is to provide coverage for the poor and those with large medical expenses by a public plan, while leaving coverage of other expenses to voluntary acquisition of private health insurance. A plan taking this approach was introduced by Senators Long and Ribicoff in 1973.

The Long-Ribicoff Bill

The Long-Ribicoff bill has three parts: (1) a catastrophic expense provision that would assist all persons covered by social security; (2) a plan to replace Medicaid by paying virtually all basic medical expenses of low-income people regardless of welfare eligibility, employment status, or family composition; and (3) provisions to promote the sale of standard health insurance policies to the nonpoor.

The catastrophic expense portion of the Long-Ribicoff bill is unchanged from the bill introduced by Senator Long earlier.[5] It would cover all medical services currently provided by Medicare (which excludes out-of-hospital drugs), but payments would be made only after sizable deductibles had been incurred. Hospital benefits would not begin until after sixty days of hospitalization, and then the plan would pick up approximately 75 percent of costs. Coverage of physicians' bills and other medical services would begin only after an annual deductible of $2,000, and individuals would pay coinsurance of 20 percent on expenses above $2,000. Coinsurance payments for covered hospital and medical services would be limited to $1,000 in a year for an individual. After that, there would be no further payment by the patient.

The catastrophic coverage would be financed by the payroll tax and coverage would be available to all families currently insured under the social security program or entitled to social security benefits. The tax rates for employers, employees, and the self-employed would be 0.30 percent for the first three years of the program, 0.35 percent for the next five years, and 0.40 percent thereafter.

The second part of the Long-Ribicoff bill would replace the Medicaid program. Eligibility would be open to all whose annual family income fell below specified amounts that vary with family size ($4,800 for a family of four) without regard to age, family status, welfare eligibility, employment, or geographical residence. Benefits include hospital care (limited to sixty days, after which expenses would be paid by the catastrophic plan), nursing-home care, physicians' services and other medical services, family planning, prenatal and well-baby care, and certain other services. Dental care, drugs, and eye and ear examinations would not be covered. Mental health benefits under the catastrophic plan would be limited to 190 days of hospital care and $250 of private practice services, but outpatient services provided by community mental health centers would be unlimited.

Patients covered by the low-income plan would make only minimal contributions toward the cost of care—for instance, $3 for each of the first

5. See Edward R. Fried and others, *Setting National Priorities: The 1974 Budget* (Brookings Institution, 1973), p. 121, for a brief discussion of the original Long bill.

ten visits to a physician. People whose income was above the cut-off would be eligible for benefits only after income net of medical expenses fell below the income limit. Thus, a family of four with an income of $4,800 could receive comprehensive medical services with a maximum payment of $30, while a similar family with an income of $6,000 and medical bills of $1,200 would be required to pay all of its own medical expenses.[6]

An estimated 24.1 million Americans would meet the income eligibility requirements of the medical assistance plan for low-income people. Another 20.1 million would receive some benefits through the "spend-down" provision that benefits those whose income net of medical outlays falls below the income limit. This part of the plan would be financed by federal and state general revenues. The state share would be equal to present Medicaid expenditures for those services covered by the plan. In addition, any state with Medicaid eligibility criteria below that of the new plan would be required to contribute one-half the payments it would have made under Medicaid if its eligibility requirements were the same as the medical assistance requirements. State contributions, therefore, would be a fixed amount that would not rise in future years.[7]

The third part of the Long-Ribicoff plan would encourage the sale of certified private insurance to defray the deductible amounts under the catastrophic expense plan.[8] Insurance companies would be asked to develop a standard policy covering the first sixty days of hospital care and at least the first $2,000 of medical expenses per person per year. The maximum deductible allowable on the hospital and medical portions would be $100 a year apiece. No further cost sharing would be permitted under the

6. Income would be defined broadly to include unearned income such as transfer payments. Income cut-offs by size of family are: $2,400 for an individual, $3,600 for a family of two, $4,200 for a family of three, and $4,800 for a family of four, plus $400 for each additional family member. Medical outlays used in calculating eligibility for those with higher incomes would include expenditures for medical services excluded from coverage.

7. State contributions would be reduced, however, by one-half of their actual expenditures for types of medical services not covered by the proposal but presently covered by Medicaid.

8. The U.S. Department of Health, Education, and Welfare would check such policies to see if they met minimum requirements for coverage, benefits, and premium charges. Premiums on group policies would have to meet some ratio to benefits paid out established by HEW, and individual policy premiums would be based on the ratio established for the smallest groups. A plan certified by HEW could use the certification emblem in its advertising. Eventually, only insurance companies selling certified plans would be eligible to serve as intermediaries or carriers under Medicare and the low-income program.

hospital plan, and total cost sharing under the medical portion could not exceed 10 percent of total expenses (or $200 on a $2,000 policy).

The Long-Ribicoff bill would also exempt insurance companies from anti-trust laws, ostensibly to permit insurers to establish insurance pools to offer certified health insurance plans. However, since the catastrophic expense plan would cover those rare claims running into tens of thousands of dollars, the need for such pooling is questionable, and the antitrust exemption might have undesirable effects on competition.

Strengths and Weaknesses of the Long-Ribicoff Approach

The Long-Ribicoff plan would be a substantial improvement over the current Medicaid program. Since the plan is a federal one with uniform benefits administered by the Social Security Administration, the extreme variations in benefits from state to state that now exist under the Medicaid program should be greatly reduced. Furthermore, by covering all low-income people, whether working or on welfare, many of the disparities in access to medical care between those on welfare and other poor people would be eliminated.

The plan, however, involves an abrupt termination of benefits as income rises above the eligibility level. While it would continue to pay some medical expenses for those with incomes just above the cut-off, each additional dollar of income earned above the limit would reduce medical benefits by one dollar. Since taxes would be paid on the additional income, the reduction in benefits would be more than 100 percent of increments to take-home pay. Given that approximately 20 million people will be affected by this provision, substantial work discentives may be expected to appear.

The bill does not require employers to purchase standard policies for employees, nor does it provide any subsidies for individuals to purchase the plan. It is doubtful, therefore, that the bill would have a substantial impact on private insurance coverage. Low-income workers, workers in small firms, and those employed in low-wage industries are likely to continue to have inadequate basic insurance coverage. In the absence of insurance to pick up the sizable deductibles of the catastrophic plan, many families could still incur severe financial burdens by trying to pay for the first sixty days of hospital care, the first $2,000 of medical bills, and as much as an additional $1,000 in cost sharing on top of the deductible amounts.

The Long-Ribicoff bill has few provisions that would help to curb increases in costs. The low-income plan includes virtually no cost sharing by patients, and the standard plan to be sold by private insurance companies does not provide for sufficient payments by patients to encourage efficiency in use of medical resources or constrain cost increases. Reimbursement to providers under the low-income plan would be on the same basis as Medicare—namely, reasonable costs and charges—and providers would be prohibited from charging those with low incomes more than the amounts established as reasonable by the Social Security Administration.

Mixed Public and Private Insurance Approaches

The administration's 1974 national health insurance plan[9] and plans sponsored by the American Hospital Association and the Health Insurance Association of America would build upon the present mix of public and private insurance to ensure access to medical care, prevent financial hardship, and control costs. Emphasis is upon filling existing gaps in the current system and eliminating the most serious shortcomings, rather than upon developing an entirely new, comprehensive system for meeting these goals.

The Administration's Approach

The administration plan contains three basic components: the employee health care insurance plan for working families, the assisted health care insurance plan for the poor, and the federal health care insurance plan to replace Medicare for the elderly.

EMPLOYEE HEALTH CARE INSURANCE PLAN. The employee health care insurance plan (EHCIP) is to be purchased by employers and employees from private insurance companies and would cover most families at an estimated premium cost of $600 per family (or $240 for an individual), at 1975 medical prices. Employers would contribute at least 65 percent of the premium cost during the first three years and 75 percent thereafter.[10] Employers also would be required to permit any employee to

9. The Ford administration did not reintroduce its plan in 1975, arguing that new expenditure programs at that time would worsen general price inflation.
10. The federal government would subsidize employers whose payroll costs increase by more than 3 percent as a result of the plan. The excess over 3 percent would be subsidized by 75 percent the first year and reduced 15 percentage points each year thereafter. Estimated cost of this subsidy is $0.45 billion during the first year.

elect a prepaid group plan and to apply the employer's portion of the premium toward it.

The benefit package is quite broad, and is identical in all three components of the plan. The benefits include hospital care, physician and other medical services, and drugs, all without limits. Family planning and maternity services and well-child care for children under six are available, as well as dental, eye, and ear care for children under thirteen. Limited mental health and posthospital care in nursing homes, and home health services are also provided.[11] Home health services are limited to one hundred visits per year, and posthospital nursing-home care is covered up to one hundred days per year.

Under the insurance plan, the family would be responsible for the first $150 of medical expenses for each family member (up to a maximum of three persons per family), the first $50 of drug expenses per person, and 25 percent of all additional expenses. Total family contributions toward medical expenses, however, would be subject to a ceiling of $1,500.[12]

Employers would be required to offer EHCIP to all full-time employees under age sixty-five and their families. Coverage is voluntary for the employee, but there are strong incentives for the employee to accept the basic plan. The employer is required to contribute at least 65 percent of the premium, and is prohibited from offering an employee any alternative coverage or contributing toward the cost of an alternative insurance plan (though the employer may offer and help pay for insurance coverage *supplementary* to the basic plan). Furthermore, the employer may not offer employees any financial inducement to decline the plan, nor may the employer make rejection of coverage under the plan a condition for employment. Because of the difficulty of enforcing these provisions, however, employers may actually give preference to secondary workers, part-time workers, or those declining insurance.

Currently, some employer health insurance plans exclude employees or dependents with serious health problems. Under the administration plan all employees and their dependents must be offered coverage without regard to their health status. An employer may not discriminate against an

11. Hospital care for the treatment of mental illness is limited to thirty days in a year (or sixty days of partial hospitalization), and physician services are limited to the cost of thirty outpatient visits if rendered in a comprehensive community care center (or the cost of 15 outpatient visits if from a private practitioner).

12. Not including any premium contribution or charges by physicians in excess of state-established reimbursement levels.

individual with respect to employment or compensation on the basis of the health status of the employee or his or her dependents.

While the administration estimates that the group premium rate for a family will be $600 in the first year, actual rates would be set by a private insurance company. It is expected, however, that competition among carriers would keep premiums at a low level in relation to the actual benefits paid for covered services. In order to ensure that group rates are not excessive for small firms with some high-risk members, each insurance company is required to offer coverage at the same premium rate to all employees in firms with up to fifty employees. This provision helps reduce the premium costs of small groups with high-risk individuals by pooling the costs among all small groups covered by a given insurance company.

The employee health care insurance plan is designed to alleviate most of the serious shortcomings of the existing system of private health insurance coverage. HEW estimates that 137 million people would have coverage under the employee plan. By setting a limit of $1,500 on family medical care costs (which will be incurred only by the few families with total medical expenses exceeding about $5,000), the financial hardship resulting from large medical bills would be greatly reduced. Requiring insurance companies to cover all workers and their families, regardless of their health, and setting a uniform premium for all small groups should make insurance coverage widely available at reasonable premium rates. Since coverage is tied to employment, however, workers changing jobs must also change insurance, thus incurring some inconvenience, cost, and possibly periods with no insurance protection.[13]

ASSISTED HEALTH CARE INSURANCE PLAN. The second part of the administration's health proposal, the assisted health care insurance plan (AHCIP), would replace most of the existing Medicaid program.[14] This plan would cover people not covered by the employee plan and those who would find its cost-sharing provisions prohibitive. The assisted plan

13. The administration plan calls for automatic coverage for ninety days following termination of employment with continuing employer contributions. The employee can then continue the coverage by paying the entire premium at the group premium rate for another ninety days. New employees would not be covered until the ninth week of full-time employment.

14. Medicaid would be retained with the current federal-state matching formula for certain services not covered by AHCIP, including: (1) services in a skilled nursing facility for patients over twenty-one, or in an intermediate care facility; (2) care in mental institutions for persons under twenty-one or over sixty-five; (3) home health services; and (4) medical or remedial care for patients in a mental institution.

would contain the same benefit package as the employee plan, but it differs in four essential ways. First, cost sharing—premiums, deductible amounts, and coinsurance rates—would be related to income, with those having lowest incomes excused from premiums and deductible amounts and subject only to low coinsurance rates. Second, physicians and other providers of medical services under the plan would be required to accept state-established reimbursement levels for services covered as payment in full. Third, the plan would be administered by the states, which would contract with private insurance carriers for AHCIP coverage. Finally, carriers would not underwrite AHCIP business but would simply be reimbursed for administrative costs.

Since the employee plan subjects low-income working families to the possibility of prohibitive medical expenses, such families might well forgo essential care even though they had insurance coverage.[15] The administration's plan gives all working families with incomes below $7,500 the option of electing coverage under AHCIP with reduced cost-sharing amounts.[16]

Families without a full-time worker would also be eligible for coverage under AHCIP, regardless of income. Realizing that the ability of such families to participate in the cost of their medical care depends crucially upon income, AHCIP relates all cost-sharing amounts to income. The premiums, deductible amounts, and coinsurance rates for each family income class, whether the family has a full-time worker or not, are shown in Table 5-2.

Since no premium is charged for families with incomes below $5,000, most low-income families, even if eligible for EHCIP, would probably elect to receive coverage under the reduced cost-sharing provisions of AHCIP.[17] Only those working families who did not clearly understand their obligations under the two plans,[18] who were apprehensive that the quality or amount of care that physicians would be willing to provide would be lower under AHCIP than under EHCIP, or who for reasons of

15. For example, a working family with an annual income of $4,000 and only moderate medical bills would face out-of-pocket payments of $500 to $700 under the employee plan. In the event of serious illness, the family would be responsible for up to $1,500 of its medical bills—plus a premium of about $200 —or 42 percent of its income.

16. Employers are required to contribute to AHCIP the premiums they would have paid if the employees had been covered under EHCIP.

17. For example, a working family with an annual income of $4,000 would be required to pay at most $360, or 9 percent of income, for medical bills, rather than as much as 42 percent of income as under the employee plan.

18. Though employers are required to explain AHCIP coverage to workers.

Table 5-2. Cost Sharing under the Assisted Health Care Insurance Plan, by Annual Family Income Class, 1975 Prices

Family income class[a] (dollars)	Amount of premium[b] (dollars)	Amount of deductible, per person (dollars)		Coinsurance rate (percent)	Maximum liability (percent of income)
		Drugs	Other[c]		
Under 2,500	0	0	0	10	6
2,500–4,999	0	25	50	15	9
5,000–7,499	300	50	100	20	12
7,500–9,999	600	50	150	25	15
10,000 and over	900	50	150	25	d

Source: H.R. 12684, 93 Cong. 2 sess., introduced February 6, 1974.

a. Income groups for single people are set at 70 percent of the family income levels.

b. For single people, the premium is zero in the first two income classes and $120, $240, and $360 in the last three classes, respectively (see note a). For full-time workers, employers also contribute the premiums they would have paid under the employee health care insurance plan, or about $390 in the first year.

c. The deductible for items other than drugs is limited to three persons per family.

d. For incomes of $10,000 and over, the maximum liability is $1,500 for a family and $1,050 for individuals.

pride preferred to be covered under the "regular" employer plan would elect coverage under EHCIP. HEW estimates that 51.1 million people would be covered by the assisted plan, while 6.5 million people would not be covered by any part of the administration plan.

Even though premiums are charged for all those with family incomes above $5,000, families who anticipate high medical expenses may purchase AHCIP coverage rather than face exorbitant premiums from individual health insurance plans. Even working families with incomes between $5,000 and $7,500 may prefer coverage under AHCIP to EHCIP if their expected medical expenses are quite high. Families with incomes above $10,000 could purchase AHCIP coverage, but only at a premium rate of $900 a year.

While the income-related cost-sharing provisions of AHCIP is the major feature distinguishing it from EHCIP, there are also important differences in administration and methods of reimbursing medical care providers and insurance companies. AHCIP is a state-administered plan, with each state contracting with private insurance companies for coverage of eligible persons. Private carriers do not underwrite AHCIP coverage; states simply compensate the carriers for any expenses in excess of premium income.[19]

19. However, if there are economies of scale in the administration of insurance, coverage of AHCIP may reduce the unit cost of administering other non-AHCIP insurance plans and hence increase the profitability of other business. Insurance companies will also have an incentive to allocate as many overhead costs to AHCIP business as possible.

Costs of AHCIP are to be borne jointly by states and the federal government, with states paying about 25 percent of the cost depending on current levels of state expenditures for Medicaid, ability to pay, and expenditures under AHCIP.

The assisted health care insurance plan corrects most of the serious inequities in the current Medicaid program. Covering all low-income people, regardless of welfare status, family composition, or employment record, should eliminate disparities in access to medical care between the poor on welfare and other low-income families. Furthermore, making the same comprehensive services available to all should greatly reduce variations in benefits across states. However, some people now covered by Medicaid would be worse off under the new plan, either because their own payments are increased slightly or because AHCIP does not cover such services as dental care for adults, private-duty nursing, and transportation services that are covered in a few states with generous Medicaid programs.[20]

FEDERAL HEALTH CARE INSURANCE PLAN. The third part of the administration's national health insurance plan would substitute the same broad benefit package provided under the employee and assisted plans for the existing Medicare program for the elderly. The plan for the elderly would be a federal program administered by the Social Security Administration. It would cover all those currently eligible for Medicare (except for the nonelderly disabled) as well as federal, state, and local government employees, and would be financed as at present by premiums and payroll tax revenues. The reduced cost sharing for the low-income elderly would be borne by federal and state general revenues. The elderly not covered by the plan would be eligible for the assisted health care plan.

Cost-sharing requirements of the federal health care insurance plan (FHCIP) are based on individual income rather than family income. Cost sharing for individual income groups is shown in Table 5-3. The premium required of those whose individual incomes are $3,500 or more—estimated to be about $90 in 1975 dollars—is similar to the Medicare premium for physician services (about $80 in fiscal 1975). The deductible of $100 would replace the current deductible of $92 for hospital care and $60 a year for physician services. The coinsurance rate of 20 percent, however, would apply to all medical services—including hospital care—and not just to physician services, as is the case with Medicare. Also unlike

20. States may elect to provide these services for the poor, even without federal support.

Table 5-3. Cost Sharing under the Federal Health Care Insurance Plan, by Annual Individual Income Class, 1975 Prices

Individual income class (dollars)	Amount of premium (dollars)	Amount of deductible, per person (dollars)		Coinsurance rate (percent)	Maximum liability (percent of income)
		Drugs	Other		
Under 1,750	0	0	0	10	6
1,750–3,499	0	25	50	15	9
3,500–5,249	90	50	100	20	12
5,250 and over	90	50	100	20	a

Source: Same as Table 5-2.
a. For incomes of $5,250 and over, the maximum liability is $750.

Medicare, FHCIP places a ceiling on payments by patients for medical services that ranges from 6 percent of income for the very poor to $750 for those with incomes of $5,250 or more.

The revised Medicare plan would eliminate many of the weaknesses in the current program. By reducing the cost-sharing requirements for all those with lower incomes, disparities in use of services among the poor should be eliminated. Instead of channeling a greater proportion of benefits to higher-income elderly people, as is the case under the physician portion of Medicare, the plan's lower deductibles would encourage lower-income people to make greater use of medical services. By making the benefit package more comprehensive (including coverage of drugs and unlimited hospitalization) and by placing a ceiling on payments by patients, many elderly people who now face severe financial hardship in meeting their share of large medical bills would be adequately protected.

However, some elderly people would be worse off under the revised plan. Those now covered by both Medicare and Medicaid may face some cost increases. Medicaid currently pays all cost-sharing amounts for the covered elderly, but under the new plan even the very poor would be required to pay 10 percent of medical bills up to a ceiling of 6 percent of individual income.[21] Higher-income elderly people facing hospital stays of moderate length would also be worse off under the new plan, since coinsurance would apply to the entire hospital stay rather than just to very long stays, as it does now. FHCIP would not cover the nonelderly disabled and those with chronic kidney disease who are now covered by Medicare. Although such patients could obtain coverage under the assisted health

21. Some states, however, may elect to pay these amounts for the elderly poor.

care insurance plan, all except the poorest of these would undoubtedly be worse off.

LIMITING COSTS UNDER THE ADMINISTRATION PLAN. The administration's proposal relies on a number of strategies to restrain increases in medical care costs. First, the benefit package under all three programs is comprehensive, thus permitting the use of lower-cost alternatives where possible. Second, the programs generally require payments by patients that would give both them and their physicians an incentive to police the market and weigh the value of various forms of treatment against the resource cost of providing the services. Third, everyone—poor, elderly, or working—could elect coverage under a health maintenance organization rather than from conventional providers of services. Such organizations are paid a fixed sum for each person covered rather than on the basis of services provided; hence, they have an incentive to use the lowest-cost combination of resources to provide any given level of care. For example, care might be more efficiently provided on an outpatient rather than an inpatient basis, by family practice physicians rather than specialists, and, where possible, by paramedical personnel rather than physicians. Health maintenance organizations with a long-term, stable enrolled population can also be expected to provide those preventive services that reduce the cost of medical care over time.[22]

Finally, the administration's plan attempts to hold down costs by its provisions for reimbursement of providers of medical services. The plan designates two types of providers: full participating providers and associate participating providers. Full participating providers would have to agree to accept state-established reimbursement levels for all treatments and types of patients.[23] Associate participating providers of care to poor and elderly patients under AHCIP and FHCIP would have to agree to accept state-established reimbursement levels as payment in full but would

22. See Charles L. Schultze and others, *Setting National Priorities: The 1973 Budget* (Brookings Institution, 1972), pp. 232–34, for a discussion of the pros and cons of health maintenance organizations.

23. Hospitals, nursing homes, and home health agencies would be required to be full participating providers, but physicians and other providers could elect to participate as associate providers. Services from full participating providers would be charged to a health card issued to each person enrolled in one of the plans. Insurance carriers would then reimburse the providers directly according to state-established levels. Patients would be billed for any cost-sharing amounts for which they are responsible and could pay over a period of time.

be free to charge other patients higher fees if their patients were notified of this practice in advance.[24]

The effectiveness of this strategy in controlling costs depends largely on the states and on the willingness of physicians to cooperate with the plan. Since state governments would be responsible for about 25 percent of the cost of the assisted plan for the poor, some states might try to limit their share of the cost by setting very restrictive reimbursement levels. This could cause many physicians to refuse to treat the poor, or physicians might attempt to subvert the restricted fee schedule by increasing the number of services offered (by giving more laboratory tests, having patients for repeat visits, limiting the length of consultations). The result could well be a system that neither effectively controls costs nor guarantees high-quality care to everyone.

There is little rationale for permitting associate participating physicians to earn larger incomes from the treatment of those covered under the employee plan than from poorer patients covered under the assisted plan, and such a reimbursement policy may well reinforce a system of two-class medicine and limit the supply of high-quality medical care available to the poor. Furthermore, permitting associate participating physicians to charge fees in excess of amounts that will be reimbursed by insurance plans may pose financial hardships for even nonpoor patients, particularly in the case of very expensive services such as complex surgery. Thus the two-part reimbursement system may undermine the national health insurance objectives of ensuring access to medical care for all and preventing the financial hardship caused by high medical bills.

The American Hospital Association Plan—The Ullman Bill

The American Hospital Association (AHA) proposal introduced by Congressman Al Ullman would also require employers to purchase a standard health insurance policy for employees and their families. Similar coverage for aged and low-income people and their families would be provided by the federal government under contract with private health insurance companies. The growth of health care corporations, which

24. Associate participating providers would have to do their own billing and collecting of fees. Providers are not prohibited from discriminating among patients on the basis of insurance status (or any other basis) and might well refuse to accept patients for whom compensation is lower.

would be charged with providing a broad range of services to enrolled members, would be promoted.

COVERAGE AND BENEFITS. Employers subject to the social security tax would be required to provide a standard health insurance plan to full-time and part-time employees.[25] Workers, however, would be free to decline coverage or select an alternative type of employer plan.

Benefits would be phased in over a five-year period. Initially, benefits would be similar to those provided in the Medicare program, plus protection against catastrophic expenses. After five years, a broad range of benefits would be offered subject to limits on numbers of services and fixed nominal copayments per unit of service. A ceiling would be placed on family out-of-pocket expenses depending upon income, age of family head, and family size. Comprehensive benefits per year include hospital care (ninety days, at $5 copayment per day), skilled nursing facility care[26] (30 days, at $2.50 per day), nursing-home care (ninety days, at $2.50 copayment per day), physicians' home, office, and outpatient center services (ten visits, at $2 copayment per visit), laboratory and X-ray services (20 percent coinsurance), home health services (one hundred visits, at $2 copayment per visit), prescription drugs for specified conditions ($1 copayment per prescription), medical equipment and prosthetic devices (20 percent coinsurance), and dental care and eyeglasses for children up to age twelve (20 percent coinsurance). Catastrophic coverage, payable when out-of-pocket expenses reach a certain amount, would cancel the cost sharing on all benefits and the limits on hospital and physicians' services.

The ceiling on family out-of-pocket expenses (including premium payments) would not exceed 10 percent of income and would be zero for families of four with incomes below $6,000. Ceilings for different income classes and family sizes are shown in Table 5-4.

This comprehensive benefit package with minimal cost sharing carries a high price tag. The estimated premium at 1975 medical prices is $1,010 per family, with the employer required to contribute at least 75 percent of the premium. However, government subsidies would be provided to cushion the impact of the high premium. Employers experiencing more than a 4 percent increase in labor costs would receive a subsidy equal to the ex-

25. If two or more members of the family were employed, coverage would be provided by the employer paying the highest wages.
26. Only facilities that are part of a hospital or are supervised by the staff of a hospital would be eligible.

Table 5-4. Maximum Liability for Out-of-Pocket Medical Expenses under the American Hospital Association Health Care Insurance Plan, by Family Size, Income Class, and Age of Head, 1975 Prices

Dollars

				Maximum liability	
Family size and income class				Family head under 65	Family head 65 and over
Single person	Family of two	Family of three	Family of four or more		
0–2,000	0–3,000	0–4,500	0–6,000	0	0
2,001–3,000	3,001–4,500	4,501–6,000	6,001–7,500	250	125
3,001–4,500	4,501–6,000	6,001–7,500	7,501–9,000	500	250
4,501–6,000	6,001–7,500	7,501–9,000	9,001–10,500	750	375
Over 6,000	Over 7,500	Over 9,000	Over 10,500	10 percent of income	

Source: Saul Waldman, *National Health Insurance Proposals: Provisions of Bills Introduced in the 93rd Congress as of July 1974*, U.S. Social Security Administration, Office of Research and Statistics, DHEW Publication (SSA) 75-11920 (1974), pp. 55, 57.

cess of the premium over the 4 percent increase, up to a maximum of ten employees. Individuals would be permitted to deduct their full premium contributions from the personal income tax (rather than one-half of the premium up to a maximum of $150, as under the current law). For those joining a health care corporation, an additional 10 percent government subsidy would be available.

The federal government would contract with private health insurance companies to provide the same broad benefit package for low-income families and the aged who are not eligible for an employee plan. This plan would replace the Medicare and most of the Medicaid program. Financing for the plan would come primarily from federal general revenues. Some premium contributions would be required for medically indigent families (with an income between $6,000 and $10,500 for a family of four). Medicare payroll tax revenues would continue to finance part of the care for the elderly. State governments would not be required to contribute to the plan.

Self-employed workers and others not covered under the employee plan and not eligible for coverage as a low-income or medically indigent family could purchase private insurance coverage at group rates through insurance pools organized by state governments.

REIMBURSEMENT OF PROVIDERS AND ADMINISTRATION OF THE PLAN. Fairly generous reimbursement schedules would be employed for both institutional and noninstitutional providers. Payment to hospitals and other institutions would be based on approved charges that would cover direct and indirect patient expenses, education and research programs, working capital and interest, "price level depreciation" for assets, capital investment expenditures in excess of depreciation, and a return on total assets. Physicians and other noninstitutional providers would be reimbursed on the basis of reasonable fees, salaries, or other compensation.

Administration of the plan would be vested in a Department of Health at the federal level and independent health commissions at the state level. A national health services advisory council and state advisory councils, to have a majority of consumer representatives, would participate in policy formulation and review proposed regulations.

HEALTH CARE CORPORATIONS. A unique feature of the American Hospital Association plan is the development of a new delivery model for health services, called a health care corporation (HCC). These nonprofit or public corporations would furnish comprehensive and coordinated health services through their own facilities or affiliated providers. Enrollment would be open to all residents of a given geographical area. A limited number of corporations would be permitted to serve each area, subject to state approval, and priority would be given to an HCC applying for an area not already served. The corporation could charge its enrollees either an annual capitation charge or a separate charge for each service, but a capitation option must eventually be made available to all who wish to enroll. The federal government would subsidize premiums or capitation fees by 10 percent for all those electing to enroll in the corporation. The federal government would assist in the development of health care corporations, especially in poverty and rural areas, by providing grants for planning and development, for new or expanded outpatient care centers, for medical equipment, data processing, and other equipment needed for initial operations, and for operating deficits during the initial phases.

LIMITATIONS OF THE AHA PLAN. The AHA plan would undoubtedly meet the goals of ensuring access to medical services for the poor and limiting the financial burden of medical care. It would do so, however, at a high cost and with great administrative complexity. It would represent a boon to the private insurance industry and to providers of medical services.

The bill is administratively complex, with detailed benefit provisions that change over time. Each type of service is subject to separate copayment requirements, but these would be forgiven for families reaching the

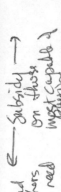

catastrophic expense limit. The ceiling would vary with income, and private insurance companies would be required to have information on the income of everyone covered under either the employee plan or the federal plan.

The plan requires only minimal cost-sharing provisions. Direct payments by patients would amount to $16 billion, compared with $23 billion under the administration's plan. The fixed copayments that are required are not tied to the price of services and hence provide no incentives for patients or their physicians to choose among alternative treatment methods or providers. The inflationary impact from increased demand would thus be substantial.

At the same time, the plan provides virtually no constraint on reimbursement of providers. Reimbursement is on the basis of approved charges and reasonable fees. Provisions for hospital reimbursement are particularly generous. The restriction of service to a limited number of health care corporations could lead to monopolistic control of the provision of health services.

Financing for the plan relies heavily on premiums. The premium income of private insurance companies would increase from $32 billion in 1975 (in the absence of a national health insurance plan) to $47 billion under this plan. The regressivity of this source of financing would be mitigated by numerous subsidies, but there would still be a heavy burden for many low-income working families. Substantial adverse employment effects could be expected from employers with a large number of low-wage full-time or part-time workers.

The Health Insurance Association of America Plan—The Burleson Bill

Unlike the administration and American Hospital Association proposals, the plan proposed by Representative Omar Burleson and endorsed by the Health Insurance Association of America (HIAA) would make selection of a standard health insurance plan voluntary for both employers and employees. Tax subsidies, however, would provide strong incentives to obtain standard coverage. Coverage of any individual or family would also be optional for insurance companies, and coverage of those considered uninsurable and the poor would be provided under state contracts.

COVERAGE AND BENEFITS. The HIAA plan also has three parts: (1) an employee plan for full-time and part-time workers; (2) an individual plan for self-employed workers and others not covered under an employee plan; and (3) a state plan for low-income families and those refused coverage at a reasonable premium under private plans.

Benefits would be the same under all three plans and would be phased in gradually over a ten-year period. Nominal fixed copayments per unit of service would be required, and coverage of most services would be limited in amount. A ceiling of $1,000 in payments for a year would be placed on family cost sharing (deductibles, copayments, and coinsurance). Comprehensive benefits would ultimately include hospital inpatient care (300 days per illness, at $5 per day), extended nursing care (180 days per illness, at $2.50 per day), physician services ($2 per visit for diagnosis or treatment, none for regularly scheduled physical examinations), and a wide range of services including dental care for all ages (20 percent copayment), eye examinations (no cost) and eyeglasses (50 percent cost sharing for those nineteen or older), prescription drugs ($1 per prescription), and physical and speech therapy (20 percent copayment).

Employers are permitted to substitute for the copayments on benefits a $100 annual deductible and 20 percent coinsurance, up to a maximum ceiling on family out-of-pocket expenses of $1,000. Assuming that most employers would select this option, HEW estimates the annual premium cost to be $920. The bill does not require employers to pay any given fraction of the premium, except that some maximums are placed on premiums to be paid by low-wage employees.[27]

Employers would not be permitted to count premium contributions as a business expense for tax purposes unless they offered a qualified plan. Employees who itemized deductions on their personal income tax returns would be permitted to deduct the full employee premium.

Individuals not covered under an employee plan would be permitted to purchase coverage from insurance pools of private insurers established by the states. These policies, however, would not contain a limit on family cost sharing. The policies would be renewable annually, but premiums would be adjusted to reflect experience under a class of policies.

The states would purchase similar coverage from private insurance companies for low-income families not covered by an employee plan and uninsurable persons (those denied coverage or offered coverage at a premium more than twice the employee rate). Families of three or more with

27. Premiums paid by employees could not exceed 10 percent of their monthly income in excess of $333 for a family of three or more, $250 for a family of two, and $167 for a single person.

incomes below $8,000 (family of two, $6,000; individual, $4,000) could voluntarily enroll in a state plan if they were not eligible under a qualified employee plan. Cost sharing would be limited to $50 a year for families with incomes below $4,000 (for a family of three or more; $3,000 and $2,000 for smaller families), graduated up to $400 for families with incomes of $8,000.

Financing of the state plans would be by premium contributions for those with incomes between $4,000 and $8,000 (maximum premium of $400). "Uninsurable" persons would pay the full actuarial premium rate. Subsidized premiums for low-income families would be met by federal and state general revenues, with the federal share ranging from 70 to 90 percent depending on the per capita income of the state. The total premium to be paid to private insurance companies for coverage of the poor would be determined by the companies and would allow for actuarial costs, costs of administration, risk charges, and repayment of any losses in past years.

The Medicare program would be retained for the elderly, but low-income families or individuals enrolled in Medicare would also be eligible for the state plan.

HEW estimates that 116 million people would be covered under the employee plan, 2 million under the individual plan, and 50 million under the state plans. An additional 24 million people would continue to be covered under Medicare. About 25 million people would not be covered under any qualified plan.

REIMBURSEMENT OF PROVIDERS AND DEVELOPMENT OF HEALTH RESOURCES. The Health Insurance Association plan would embody a more conservative method of reimbursement of providers than the American Hospital Association plan. Payments to health care institutions would be based on prospectively approved rates, after budgets submitted to state cost commissions had been reviewed. Charges would be required to be reasonably related to the cost of efficient production of services. Physicians, dentists, and other noninstitutional providers would also be paid on the basis of reasonable charges, taking into account the customary charge of the practitioner and the prevailing charge in the area. Payment could not exceed the seventy-fifth percentile of the distribution of actual charges in the previous year.

The HIAA plan contains a number of provisions that would try to ensure the availability of medical resources. One provision subsidizes development of comprehensive ambulatory health care centers, particularly in densely populated areas without such facilities. Loans to students in a wide range of health and allied professions would be increased. Grants would be provided to professionals agreeing to serve in areas of critical need and to health training schools that emphasize staffing of ambulatory health care centers.

LIMITATIONS OF THE HIAA PLAN. The HIAA plan shares many of the flaws of the other approaches that rely heavily on private insurance. Premiums are a major source of financing, and though coverage is voluntary, it shifts a major share of the burden to low-income working families, who could well come to resent the lower premiums and cost sharing required of families with the same incomes but not covered by employee plans.

The plan would also perpetuate many of the flaws of current private health insurance coverage. Poor health risks would be excluded from employee plans and required to pay a premium that reflected their high expected expenditures. Extensive coverage of hospital care would be continued and increased. Broad coverage of ambulatory services could be quite inflationary as many previously uncovered or only partially covered services came under insurance.

Not surprisingly, the plan would be quite favorable to the private insurance industry. Premium income from employee and individual plans would increase from $32.5 billion in the absence of national health insurance to $40 billion under this plan. In addition, firms would be permitted to earn some return on the $23 billion of insurance coverage provided to low-income families by states.

Payments to providers of medical services are more limited than under some other proposals, but patients would be required to pay physician charges that exceed those established as reimbursable under the plan.

Public Insurance Approaches

Unlike the plans discussed above, there are two major bills that would provide greater public control over the provision of national health insurance—a compromise bill sponsored by Senator Kennedy and Congressman Mills, and the Health Security Act, originally introduced by Senator Kennedy and Congresswoman Griffiths and supported by the AFL-CIO. About 70 percent of personal health care expenditures would be publicly financed under the Kennedy-Mills bill (K-M) and almost 90 percent under the Health Security Act, in contrast to all the other major proposals, in which the public share would not exceed 45 percent.[28]

The Kennedy-Mills Bill

Although the Kennedy-Mills bill differs from the administration plan in that it is primarily a public plan, financed from tax revenues rather than premium contributions, its benefits are similar to those of the administration's plan. The range of benefits covered is the same, although the K-M bill would provide more limited prescription drug benefits.

Cost sharing under the K-M plan, however, is more limited than under the administration plan. All services other than preventive ones (family planning, prenatal and well-child care, and dental, eye, and ear care for children) would be subject to a per-person deductible of $150, not to exceed two persons per family (rather than three persons as in the administration plan). All services, except drugs, would also be subject to a 25 percent coinsurance payment; for drugs there would be a separate copayment of $1 per prescription.

A maximum ceiling, however, is set on each family's contribution. For families with incomes above $8,800, the ceiling would be $1,000 (rather than $1,500 as in the administration plan). No payments would be required for families of four with incomes below $4,800. For families with incomes between $4,800 and $8,800, the maximum ceiling is increased by $250 for each $1,000 of income over $4,800. As shown in Table 5-5, low-income families would face substantially lower maximum payments under the K-M plan than under the administration's assisted plan.

While there are substantial differences between the maximum payments required under the two plans, few middle-income families would actually have to make the maximum payments. Differences in average payments would be substantially less. For example, consider a typical family of four, where one member incurs $750 of medical expenses, a second member $150, and the other two $50 each (with no drug or preventive care expenses). Out-of-pocket expenses for such a family under the two plans are shown in Figure 5-1. Family payments are virtually the same for incomes above $7,500, but substantially less under the Kennedy-Mills plan for low-income families. Benefits decline much more rapidly with income in the Kennedy-Mills plan, however, as families with incomes slightly

---

28. These percentages include payments for Medicare, Medicaid, and other public programs if retained under the plan.

Table 5-5. Maximum Liability for Out-of-Pocket Medical Expenses under the Administration Assisted Health Care Insurance Plan and the Kennedy-Mills Plan, by Selected Family Incomes, 1975 Prices

| | Maximum family liability[a] | | | |
| | Administration assisted plan | | Kennedy-Mills plan[b] | |
Family income (dollars)	Amount (dollars)	Percent of income	Amount (dollars)	Percent of income
2,000	120	6	0	0
4,000	360	9	0	0
5,000	600	12	50	1
6,000	720	12	300	5
8,000	1,200	15	800	10
10,000	1,500	15	1,000	10

Source: Same as Table 5-4, pp. 33, 166.
a. A separate schedule applies to individuals.
b. For a family of four. The figures vary with family size.

above $4,800 find medical benefits reduced by 25 cents for each additional dollar of income.

Responsibility for administration of the K-M national health insurance plan would be vested in the Social Security Administration, which would be reestablished as an independent agency outside of HEW. Private insurance companies would administer the payment for SSA; however, employers with 1,000 or more employees could choose the insurer (among those under contract with SSA) to administer their programs. Just as in the administration plan, every insured individual would be issued a health card and a health card account would be established for each enrollee for charging medical services from participating providers. Providers would be paid by the SSA on the basis of the accounts, and patients would be billed directly from the accounts by the SSA for deductible and coinsurance amounts.

Financing for the program would come from a combination of payroll taxes, taxes on unearned income, and federal and state general revenues. A 4 percent payroll tax on employment earnings up to $20,000 a year would be shared by employers and employees, with the employer responsible for at least 3 percent. Self-employed individuals would pay a single rate of 2.5 percent up to $20,000 on their covered earnings. For those with annual earnings or self-employment income of less than $20,000, a tax of 2.5 percent on any unearned income, up to a combined total of $20,000, would be assessed. A family with interest, rent, and dividend

Figure 5-1. Cost Sharing for a Family of Four with $1,000 in Annual Medical
Expenses under the Administration's Assisted Health Care and the
Kennedy-Mills Plans, 1975 Prices

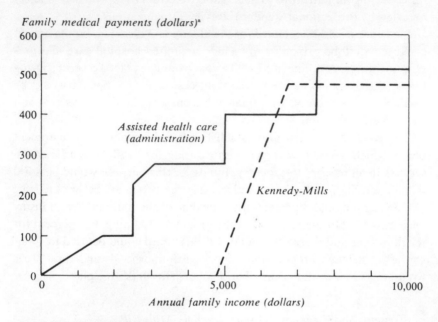

Family medical payments (dollars)[a]

*Assisted health care
(administration)*

Kennedy-Mills

Annual family income (dollars)

Source: Same as Table 5-4, pp. 33, 166.
a. Excluding premiums for health insurance.

income of $20,000 but with no earnings or self-employment income, for
example, would be required to pay $500. Income from transfer payments
would also be taxable as unearned income, except that benefits from the
Aid to Families with Dependent Children and the supplemental security
income programs would be taxed at the rate of 1 percent on the recipient
(which would be withheld) and 3 percent on the state. Reduced cost
sharing for low-income families would be met from federal general revenues plus a continuing contribution from the states equal to their 1973
Medicaid expenditures or their 3 percent contributions for AFDC and
SSI families, whichever was higher.

The K-M plan makes elaborate provisions for controlling the cost of
health care. Institutional providers would be reimbursed by prospective
payment systems with various incentive features. Physicians and other
professionals would be reimbursed according to fee schedules established
by the professions but adjusted by the SSA according to price and earn-

ing changes in the economy. Physicians could charge any patient more than the established fee schedule allowed but would then be responsible for collecting all patient payments. All covered services would be subject to review by Professional Standards Review Organizations.

Medicare would be retained for the elderly and disabled, but its benefit package would be expanded to include unlimited hospital care and prescription drugs. A ceiling of $1,000 a year would be placed on cost sharing for an elderly family. A new long-term custodial care benefit would be available to the elderly, with financing from premiums and federal and state general revenues.

The K-M plan would also establish a health resources development board, which would be charged with assuring the availability of medical services in all parts of the country. Funds for this purpose would be $400 million and $600 million, respectively, for the two years before the start of the program, and 2 percent of the income of the national health insurance trust fund in the first year of the program, declining to 1 percent for the third year and thereafter. Funds for this board could be used to sponsor health delivery programs in minority neighborhoods and rural areas to ensure a more equitable distribution of benefits under the plan.

Strengths and Weaknesses of the Kennedy-Mills Bill

The Kennedy-Mills bill would create one system with uniform benefits and coverage for nearly all nonelderly U.S. citizens. By requiring consumer payments that vary with income and contributions by the states, it would limit the revenues that would be required from increases in federal taxes, and it would concentrate budgetary resources on those with the greatest need for financial assistance—the poor and those with large medical bills. It would greatly reduce potential variations in benefits among states by establishing a single federal reimbursement policy rather than permitting separate reimbursement policies for each state. The intermediate role for private insurance companies proposed would neither greatly increase the profitability of the industry nor eliminate it entirely.

Perhaps the most serious deficiency of the plan is its potential impact on costs. Since physicians are permitted to charge all patients more than the federally established reimbursement levels, they will undoubtedly take advantage of the increased insurance to charge higher fees. If, as apparently happened with Medicare, physicians respond to their increased incomes by working fewer hours, the total amount of medical services supplied may, in fact, decline. It is somewhat ironic that the Kennedy-Mills bill provides this escape clause for physicians while at the same time establishing an elaborate mechanism for determining reimbursement schedules.

Another potential problem is the complexity of the review procedures established by the plan. All services would be subject to review by professional organizations for their necessity and appropriateness, a procedure that could prove to be quite cumbersome. Finally, the bill does not eliminate tax subsidies that encourage the purchase of supplementary insurance, thus mitigating those market forces that help to constrain costs.

The Health Security Act—The Kennedy-Griffiths Bill

The Health Security Act would replace the existing system of private insurance coverage and public programs for the poor and elderly with a single, comprehensive federal system. Under the Kennedy-Griffiths bill, the entire population would be covered for a broad range of health services with no payments whatsoever required of the patient. In addition, the proposal includes provisions designed to reorganize the delivery of health services, improve health planning, and increase the supply of health care manpower and facilities.

Financing for the plan would come from taxes on payrolls and self-employed and unearned income, and from federal general revenues. No state contributions would be required. Tax rates would be 1.0 percent on employee wages and unearned income, 3.5 percent for employers, and 2.5 percent for the self-employed. Federal general revenues would match total receipts from taxes on payroll, self-employment, and unearned income. Income subject to the tax on earnings would be $15,000 annually for individuals, and the entire payroll for the employer's contribution; the tax base for individuals would be automatically adjusted upward to be 125 percent of the regular social security payroll tax earnings base.

Because the Kennedy-Griffiths program would provide free medical care to all, with no deductibles or coinsurance, control of excessive use and medical care price inflation would have to be exercised through a series of financial and regulatory devices. Each year a national medical care budget for the coming year would be established, based on the current year's cost and estimated changes in prices, population, and supply of medical providers. That fixed budget would then be allocated to regions, and within the regions to health service areas. Physicians and other professionals could elect to be paid on a capitation, fixed salary, or fee-for-service basis, though the program is designed to discourage the fee-for-service option. Health maintenance organizations providing all services on a capitation basis would be given preferential treatment. Each hospital would have to operate within a fixed budget.

Strengths and Weaknesses of the Health Security Act

The plan would meet the objectives of removing financial barriers to medical care for the poor and preventing financial hardships from high medical bills for all. By establishing one system for everyone with a uniform reimbursement policy, the plan would go a long way toward eliminating two-class medical care. Furthermore, the federal government, by being the sole source of financing for medical care services, would have tremendous leverage to control medical care costs, encourage more efficient forms of organizing and delivering services, and influence the distribution and availability of medical manpower and facilities.

The absence of any consumer payments under the Kennedy-Griffiths plan, however, creates a number of difficulties. It greatly increases the cost of the plan to the federal government, and hence the taxes that must be raised to finance it. In the absence of any consumer payments and automatic market incentives, all decisions regarding reimbursement, proper utilization of services, appropriate allocation of resources, and so forth, must be made by regulatory bodies. Finally, making care available free of charge to everyone may well cause greater utilization of medical care services by high-income people, at the expense of those more in need of care: since physicians tend to be more heavily concentrated in high-income areas, residents of such areas would logically generate the greatest increases in demand. Thus, the result of providing free medical care to all might paradoxically be to increase care most for those who can already afford it.

Summary

Perhaps the most striking similarity among the major national health insurance bills before Congress is their emphasis on a comprehensive range of health services. All plans cover both inhospital and ambulatory services. Most provide at least limited skilled nursing-home benefits and coverage of prescription drugs. Some include dental care, at least for children, and other preventive services for pregnant women and young children.

All the plans would cover most of the population. The Health Security Act and the Long-Ribicoff bill are similar in that both would cover the entire population,[29] although the former would provide comprehensive benefits with no patient cost sharing while the latter would provide limited catastrophic benefits with substantial patient payments. Under the other plans, however, some small fraction of the population would remain uncovered. As shown in Table 5-6, 3 million people would not be reached by the Kennedy-Mills bill, while 25 million (mostly the self-employed, workers in small firms, and poor health risks) would not have standard private insurance under the Health Insurance Association of America plan.

Direct payments required of patients would range from $10 billion under the Health Security Act (mostly for noncovered services such as some nursing-home care, nonprescription drugs, eyeglasses, and appliances) to $28 billion under the Long-Ribicoff bill (see Table 5-6). Under most bills, payments by the poor are either not required or quite low. The Long-Ribicoff bill would require patient payments representing a high fraction of income by many lower-income working families (those with incomes between $5,000 and $10,000). Patient payments under the Health Security Act and the American Hospital Association plan are too low to act as important sources of cost constraint. The American Medical Association plan, while providing for $21 billion of direct payments by patients, has very limited direct payments for hospital and physician care. Most patient payments under that plan are for noncovered services.

Major differences exist among the bills in the sources of financing. Premium contributions would be highest in the administration bill and those of the trade associations (American Medical Association, American Hospital Association, and Health Insurance Association of America), representing 50 percent or more of all financing. Premiums as a source of financing would be used to only a limited extent—mostly for medical care of the elderly—under the Long-Ribicoff and Kennedy-Mills plans. As shown in Table 5-6, state government contributions would range from 2

29. Coverage under Long-Ribicoff is limited to those persons insured, or receiving benefits, under social security.

Table 5-6. Coverage, Financing, and Type of Provider Reimbursement under Alternative National Health Insurance Plans, Based on Prices and Population Projected for 1975

Item	No national health insurance plan	Supporter or sponsor of plan						
		American Medical Association	Long-Ribicoff	Administration	American Hospital Association	Health Insurance Association of America	Kennedy-Mills	Health Security Act (AFL-CIO)
Persons not covered by the plan (millions)	...	4.0	0	6.5	8.3	25.0	3.0	0
Direct patient payments[a] (billions of dollars)	30.1	21.1	28.1	22.7	16.1	21.9	20.3	9.9
Sources of financing[b] (as percent of total cost of plan)								
Premiums	6.0	57.8	4.5	51.8	53.5	50.1	4.6	0
Federal funds	71.5	37.1	76.4	38.3	44.1	41.8	88.8	98.0
State funds	22.4	5.1	19.0	9.9	2.4	8.1	6.6	2.0
Private health insurance business[c] (billions of dollars)								
Income from sales	32.5	62.3	30.9	37.3	47.4	62.5[d]	11.7	3.0
Administered claims and expenses	22.0	13.7	37.8	41.8	43.4	13.7	71.5	0
Extent of reimbursement of providers (in relation to total cost)	...	Unrestricted	Medicare type	Moderate	Generous	Medicare type[e]	Moderate	Restricted

Sources: From or estimated from U.S. Department of Health, Education, and Welfare, *Estimated Health Expenditures under Selected National Health Insurance Bills, A Report to the Congress* (1974). Figures are rounded.

a. Direct payments by patients do not include premiums for coverage by the plan or for supplementary insurance coverage.

b. Sources of financing include payments for the plan and for Medicare and Medicaid if they are retained under the plan. Medicare and Medicaid expenditures, in case there is no national health insurance, are shown under no plan. Other public expenditures, premiums for supplementary private insurance coverage, and direct patient payments are not included.

c. Private health insurance industry includes both national health insurance and any supplementary alternative private health insurance. Premiums paid into public plans, such as Medicare, are counted as administered claims rather than sales.

d. The Health Insurance Association of America plan calls for $22.5 billion of insurance for lower-income families to be sold; however, some limits are placed on the rates of return that can be earned on the sale of insurance to the poor.

e. Includes prospective budgets for hospitals.

percent of all revenues under the Health Security Act to 19 percent in the Long-Ribicoff proposal. Federal expenditures would account for over 75 percent of total financing under the Long-Ribicoff and Kennedy-Mills plans and the Health Security Act.

The bills would also have varying impacts on the private health insurance industry. The trade association bills would increase sales of private health insurance from $32 billion to between $45 and $65 billion. The Health Security Act would virtually eliminate private insurance, while the Kennedy-Mills bill would limit sales of insurance to about $12 billion. Private health insurance companies would be involved in administering coverage for the poor under all plans except the Health Security Act.

The only bills to develop major roles for consumers are the American Hospital Association bill, the Kennedy-Mills bill, and the Health Security Act, which have provisions for consumers to serve as members of advisory councils. Most bills are silent, or vague, as to safeguards on individual privacy and methods for determining income in income-related plans.

A variety of methods of reimbursing providers of medical services is to be found in the bills, ranging from the virtually unrestricted methods of paying providers in the American Medical Association bill to the fairly stringent curbs on payments under the Health Security Act. Most bills favor moderate methods of reimbursement, which attempt to leave physicians and hospitals with about the same average level of reimbursement as they currently earn. The administration and Kennedy-Mills bills would try new methods of reimbursement, while the Long-Ribicoff bill would model reimbursement along the same lines as used in the Medicare program.

Most of the bills do not contain automatic adjustments of the income requirements for eligibility or the amount of payments by patients over time. Tax subsidies for the purchase of private insurance are retained under all bills and substantially increased in several.

Tables 5-7 through 5-13 summarize each of the major bills with respect to coverage, benefits, methods of administration and financing, standards and reimbursement of providers of services, and any provisions relating to the delivery, organization, or development of health resources.

Table 5-7. Major Features of the Health Care Insurance Plan Supported by the American Medical Association, 1974

Item	Provisions
General concept and approach	A program that would allow credits against personal income taxes to offset the premium cost of approved private health insurance with specified benefits. It would also require employers to offer approved policies to retain favorable tax treatment.
Coverage of the population	All U.S. residents, on a voluntary basis.
Benefit structure	Tax credits of 10 to 100 percent of the cost of an approved health insurance policy, depending on annual tax payments. Voucher certificates would be issued to persons with little or no tax liability. *Institutional services:* hospital up to sixty days of care, with a $50 deductible per stay; skilled nursing facility care could be substituted for hospital care on the basis of two days for every one, with a $50 deductible per stay. *Personal services:* physicians, 20 percent coinsurance; dentists for children aged two to six (eventually to be extended to age seventeen); home health care, 20 percent coinsurance; laboratory and X-ray, 20 percent coinsurance. *Other services and supplies:* ambulance, 20 percent coinsurance. *Catastrophic coverage:* unlimited hospital days, an additional thirty days in a skilled nursing facility, prosthetic devices, and blood (above three pints) covered after out-of-pocket payment, which would vary according to income. *Total coinsurance:* limited to $100 per family for physicians, laboratory, and X-ray combined; separate limit of $100 for hospital outpatient care, home health care, and ambulance; and separate limit of $100 for dentists. Medicaid would pay all cost sharing for cash assistance recipients.
Administration	Private insurance carriers would issue health insurance policies. State insurance departments would certify carriers and approved policies. The U.S. Department of Health, Education, and Welfare would issue voucher certificates. A new federal board would establish standards for the program.
Relationship to other government programs	*Medicare:* would continue to operate. *Medicaid and related programs:* would not pay for services covered under these programs. *Other programs:* most not affected.
Financing	Tax credits financed from federal general revenues. Employers must provide approved policies as a condition of taking the full premium cost as a normal business deduction.

Table 5-7. (*Continued*)

Item	Provisions
Standards for providers of services	No provisions.
Reimbursement of providers of services	Usual and customary charges.
Delivery and resources	No provisions.

Source: Same as Table 5-4, p. 17.

Table 5-8. Major Features of the Long-Ribicoff Catastrophic Health Insurance and Medical Assistance Reform Plan, 1974

	Provisions	
Item	Catastrophic plan	Medical assistance plan
General concept and approach	A two-part program including: (1) a catastrophic illness plan for the general population, and (2) a federal medical assistance plan for the poor and medically indigent. Both plans would be administered through the Medicare program. The plan also includes provisions designed to encourage the improvement of private health insurance and the establishment of insurance pools.	
Coverage of the population	Persons of all ages covered by or receiving benefits under social security.	Families with income below specified amounts, which vary by family size, regardless of age or employment status of head. Would also cover families with income above the specified limits under a "spend-down" provision that would take into account both family income and medical expenses. Those now eligible for Medicaid would automatically be covered.
Benefit structure	Same types of benefits as Medicare, but payable only when expenses reached specified catastrophic proportions. *Institutional services:* hospital coverage to begin after first sixty days of care, with no limit on additional days covered, $21 per day copayment; skilled nursing facility up to 100 days, $10.50 per day copayment, available only to those who had received catastrophic hospital benefits. *Personal services* (payable after a family has incurred $2,000 in medical expenses in a year; 20 percent coinsurance): physicians; laboratory and X-ray; home health care. *Other services* (with the same requirements as for personal services): medical supplies and appliances; ambulance. *Total coinsurance:* limited to $1,000 annually per person.	No limits on amount of services and no cost sharing, except as indicated below. *Institutional services:* hospital up to sixty days; skilled nursing facility; intermediate care facility. *Personal services:* physicians, $3 per visit copayment for first ten visits per family; laboratory and X-ray; home health care. *Other services and supplies:* medical supplies and appliances; ambulance. Plan would also pay full cost of benefits under the catastrophic plan for medical assistance recipients not covered by it, and the required cost sharing for those who are covered. It would also pay the supplemental medical insurance premium of Medicare for the eligible aged.

Table 5-8. (*Continued*)

Item	Provisions	
	Catastrophic plan	*Medical assistance plan*
Administration	Administered through the Medicare program, under which private carriers would handle claims and pay providers of services.	
Relationship to other government programs	*Medicare:* would continue to operate. *Medicaid:* would pay last. *Other programs:* most not affected.	*Medicare:* would continue to operate. *Medicaid:* abolished. *Other programs:* most not affected.
Financing	As under Medicare, special tax on the wages and self-employment income subject to the social security tax. The tax rate would initially be 0.3 percent, rising ultimately to 0.4 percent.	Financed by state and federal general revenues. The state share would be an amount equal to the present state share of Medicaid payments for the types of services offered under the new program, with additions or subtractions depending on its present Medicaid program. The federal share would be the balance of the cost.
Standards for providers of services	Same as under Medicare.	Same as under Medicare. In addition, intermediate care facilities must be licensed by the states and meet additional requirements.
Reimbursement of providers of services	Same as under Medicare, including the reimbursement provision of P.L. 92-603.	Same as under Medicare, except that physicians and other providers must accept the plan's payment as payment in full.
Delivery and resources	Incorporates the provisions of P.L. 92-603, including the establishment of health maintenance organizations and Professional Standards Review Organizations. The plan also encourages the improvement of private insurance in the following ways. Private carriers could voluntarily submit health insurance policies for certification by the U.S. Department of Health, Education, and Welfare. An emblem of certification could be used by them in advertising, and only approved carriers could act as Medicare intermediaries. A certified policy would have to (1) include specified benefits (sixty days of hospital care and $2,000 medical coverage), with limitations on cost sharing; (2) not exclude preexisting conditions; and (3) for employment group policies, continue coverage for terminated employees. The plan also suspends certain antitrust laws, thus permitting insurance "pool" arrangements to offer certified insurance.	

Source: Same as Table 5-4, p. 22.

Table 5-9. Major Features of the National Health Insurance Plan Supported by the Administration, 1974

Item	Provisions		
	Employee plan	*Assisted plan*	*Plan for the aged*
General concept and approach	A three-part program including: (1) a plan requiring employers to provide private health insurance for employees, (2) an assisted plan for low-income and high-medical-risk people, and (3) an improved federal Medicare program for the aged. The states would supervise providers of health services and insurance carriers under federal guidelines.		
Coverage of the population	Full-time employees, including employees of state and local governments.	Low-income families, employed or unemployed, and families and employment groups that are high medical risks.	Aged people covered by social security.
Benefit structure	No limits on benefits, except as indicated below. *Institutional services:* hospital, inpatient and outpatient; skilled nursing facility up to 100 days per year. *Personal services:* physicians; dentists for children under thirteen; laboratory and X-ray; home health care up to 100 visits per year; family planning, maternity care, and well-child care for children under six, by regulation. *Other services and supplies:* prescription drugs; medical supplies and appliances; eyeglasses and hearing aids (and eye and ear examinations) for children under thirteen.		
Cost sharing	Deductible of $150 per person and 25 percent coinsurance, but total cost sharing is limited to $1,500 annually per family or $1,050 for individuals.	Maximum cost-sharing provisions are same as under employee plan, but amount is reduced according to individual or family income.	Deductible of $100 per person and 20 percent coinsurance, but total cost sharing is limited to $750 per person annually. Cost sharing is reduced according to individual income for low-income aged.
Administration	Insurance offered by private carriers (or self-insured arrangements) supervised by the states under federal regulations.	Administered by the states, using private carriers to administer benefits, under federal regulations.	Administered by the federal government in a manner similar to the present Medicare program.

Table 5-9. (*Continued*)

Item	Provisions		
	Employee plan	*Assisted plan*	*Plan for the aged*
Relationship to other government programs	*Medicare:* would continue to operate. *Medicaid:* no federal matching funds for covered benefits, premiums, or cost sharing under the new program, but it would continue for specified noncovered services such as intermediate care facilities.		
Financing	Employer-employee premium payments, with employer paying 75 percent (65 percent for first three years). Temporary federal subsidies for employers with unusually high increases in payroll costs. Special provisions to assure coverage for small employers.	Premium payments from enrollees according to family income (zero for lowest-income groups). Balance of costs to be met by federal and state general revenues, with state share varying according to state per capita income.	Continuation of present Medicare payroll taxes and premium payments by the aged, but with no premiums for low-income people. Federal and state general revenues would finance reduced cost sharing and premiums for low-income aged.
Standards for providers of services	Similar to those under Medicare, with additional standards for paramedical personnel.		
Reimbursement of providers of services	Reimbursement rates would be established by the states, according to federal procedures and criteria. Providers who elect as "full participating" would receive the state-established rates, including any cost sharing, as full payment. Providers who elect as "associate participating" could charge more than the state rate for employee-plan patients, but would have to collect the extra charges and cost-sharing amounts from the patients. All hospitals and skilled nursing facilities would have to be full participating providers.		
Delivery and resources	*Prepaid practice plans:* the option would be available of enrolling in approved prepaid group or individual practice plans that met special standards. *Regulation of insurance carriers:* regulated by the states, including approval of premium rates, enforcement of disclosure requirements, annual audit by certified public accountants, and protection against the insolvency of carriers. *Regulation of providers:* regulated by the states, including standards for participation in the program, approval of proposed capital expenditures, and enforcement of disclosure requirements. *Professional Standards Review Organization:* would apply to all services under the program and extend provisions to both outpatient and inpatient services.		

Source: Same as Table 5-4, p. 4.

Table 5-10. Major Features of the National Health Care Services Plan Supported by the American Hospital Association, 1974

	Provisions	
Item	*Private plan*	*Plan for the low-income and aged*
General concept and approach	A three-part program covering the entire population, including: (1) a plan requiring employers to provide private coverage for employees, (2) a plan for individuals, and (3) federally contracted coverage for the poor and aged. States would establish a health care plan, supervise carriers and insurers, and promote a system of chartered health care corporations (HCCs).	
Coverage of the population	Employees (and their families) of employers subject to the social security tax, plus individuals who elect coverage.	Low-income and medically indigent families and the aged.
Benefit structure	Benefits would be phased in over a five-year period. Final benefits as follows: *Institutional services:* hospital up to ninety days, $5 per day copayment; skilled nursing facility up to thirty days, $2.50 per day copayment; nursing home up to ninety days, $2.50 per day copayment. *Personal services:* physicians up to ten visits per year, $2 per visit copayment; dentists for children aged seven to twelve, for one examination per year, with 20 percent coinsurance for other services; laboratory and X-ray, 20 percent coinsurance; home health care up to 100 visits per year, $2 per visit copayment. *Other services and supplies:* prescription drugs limited to specified conditions, $1 per prescription copayment; medical supplies and appliances, 20 percent coinsurance; ambulance, 20 percent coinsurance; eyeglasses (one set per year) for children up to twelve, 20 percent coinsurance. *Catastrophic coverage:* payable when certain noncovered expenses reached a specified limit, which would vary by family income and age of head. It would remove the cost sharing on all benefits and the limitation on the number of hospital days and visits to physicians covered.	
Administration	Administered by private insurance carriers under state supervision, according to federal guidelines.	The federal government would contract with private insurance carriers, which would issue policies to eligible persons.
Relationship to other government programs	*Medicare:* abolished. *Medicaid and related programs:* would not pay for services covered under these programs. *Other programs:* most not affected.	

Table 5-10. (*Continued*)

Item	Provisions	
	Private plan	*Plan for the low-income and aged*
Financing	By employee-employer premium payments, with the employer paying at least 75 percent. There would be a federal subsidy of the premium for low-income workers and certain small employers, and a 10 percent subsidy for HCC enrollees. Individuals would pay their own premiums.	Financed in part by premium payments by medically indigent, but with no premium for the lowest-income group. Balance of the cost to be financed by federal general revenues and the portion of payroll taxes assigned to the present Medicare program.
Standards for providers of services	All institutions and HCCs must meet Medicare standards. Skilled nursing facilities must be under the supervision of hospital medical staffs or have their own organized staffs. Use of paramedical personnel must meet federal standards. All providers and HCCs must establish systems of peer review, medical audit, and other procedures to meet federal and state requirements on quality and utilization of services.	
Reimbursement of providers of services	*Institutions and HCCs:* state commissions would approve charges based on review of budget and schedule of proposed charges. *Physicians and other professionals:* on the basis of a reasonable fee, salary, or other compensation, as approved by state commissions.	
Delivery and resources	*State health commissions:* would establish a state health plan, including provisions for regulation of providers and insurance carriers, take responsibility for health planning, and approve in advance proposed capital expenditures of providers. *Health care corporations:* state commissions would incorporate system of HCCs to operate in designated geographical areas. An HCC would furnish all covered services through its own facilities or affiliated providers and would permit all qualified practitioners to furnish services for it. It would be required to hold open enrollment for the public and eventually offer services on a per capita basis. HCCs would receive federal grants for planning, development, outpatient centers, medical and data equipment, and to cover initial operating deficits.	

Source: Same as Table 5-4, p. 5.

Table 5-11. Major Features of the National Health Insurance Plan Supported by the Health Insurance Association of America, 1974

Item	*Provisions*	
	Private plan	*State plan*
General concept and approach	A three-part voluntary health insurance plan including: (1) an employee-employer plan, (2) a plan for individuals, and (3) a state plan for the poor. All plans would be administered through private insurance carriers and provide the same benefits.	
Coverage of the population	Employees (and their families) of employers who voluntarily elect coverage under a qualified plan, plus individuals who elect coverage.	Poor and uninsurable persons.
Benefit structure	Benefits would be phased in over a ten-year period for private plans and a five-year period for state plan. Final benefits as follows: *Institutional services:* hospital up to 300 days, $5 per day copayment; skilled nursing facility up to 180 days, $2.50 per day copayment. *Personal services:* physicians, $2 per visit copayment; dentists, one examination per year, 20 percent coinsurance for other services; laboratory and X-ray, no cost sharing; home health care up to 270 days, $2.50 per day copayment; other health professionals, 20 percent coinsurance. *Other services and supplies:* prescription drugs, $1 per prescription copayment; medical appliances, 20 percent coinsurance; eyeglasses, no coinsurance for children under nineteen, 50 percent coinsurance for all others.	
Cost sharing	Under employee-employer plan, an annual limit of $1,000 per family for all cost sharing. Under individual plans, no limit on cost sharing.	No cost sharing for lowest-income families; for others, cost sharing would vary according to family income.
Administration	Administered by private carriers under state supervision. Treasury Department would determine tax status of the plan.	Administered by private carriers under agreement with the states. Regulations for program would be established by the U.S. Department of Health, Education, and Welfare.
Relationship to other government programs	*Medicare:* would continue to operate. *Medicaid and related programs:* would not pay for services covered under these programs. *Other programs:* most not affected.	

Table 5-11. (*Continued*)

Item	Provisions	
	Private plan	*State plan*
Financing	Under employee-employer plan, premium paid by employers and employees, as arranged between them, but with the contributions of low-income workers limited according to their wage level. Under individual plan, policyholder would pay entire premium. Employees and individuals who itemize deductions on their income tax returns could deduct entire premium. Employers could take their entire premium as a normal business deduction, but contributions to nonqualified plans would not be deductible.	No premium required for lowest-income group; for others, premium paid by enrollees, with the amount varying according to family income. Federal and state governments would pay the balance of the cost from their general revenues, with the federal share ranging from 70 to 90 percent, depending on the state.
Standards for providers of services	Same as under Medicare.	
Reimbursement of providers of services	*Hospitals and other institutions:* rates for various categories of institutions would be approved by state commissions (subject to HEW review of rate levels) on the basis of a review of budgets and schedule of charges. *Physicians and dentists:* on the basis of reasonable charges, based on prevailing rates.	
Delivery and resources	*Health planning:* increased funding for state and local planning agencies, whose approval would be required for projects receiving federal assistance. *Health maintenance organizations:* must be made available as an option to persons enrolled in state or employee-employer plans. *Ambulatory health centers:* would receive grants, loans, and loan guarantees for the construction and operation of centers. *Manpower training:* increased loans and grants for students, with special provisions for shortage areas.	

Source: Same as Table 5-4, p. 7.

Table 5-12. Major Features of the Kennedy-Mills National Health Insurance Plan, 1974

Item	Provisions		
	National health insurance	*Medicare, regular*	*Medicare, long-term benefits*
General concept and approach	A two-part program including: (1) a national health insurance plan for the general population, and (2) a revised Medicare program for the aged and disabled, including a new long-term care benefit plan. Both programs would be administered by an independent Social Security Administration. The plan includes provisions for improving health resources and delivery.		
Coverage of the population	Persons insured or eligible under social security, working full time, or under the Aid to Families with Dependent Children or supplemental security income program.	Same as present Medicare program for the aged and disabled.	
Benefit structure	No limits on benefits, except as indicated below. *Institutional services:* hospital inpatient and outpatient; skilled nursing facility up to 100 days per year. *Personal services:* physicians; dentists for children under thirteen; laboratory and X-ray; home health care up to 100 visits per year; family planning, maternity care, and well-child care for children under six, by regulation. *Other services and supplies:* prescription drugs for specified chronic illnesses; medical supplies and appliances; eyeglasses and hearing aids (and eye and ear examinations) for children under thirteen.		Home health care. Homemaker services. Meals-on-wheels. Outpatient mental health services. Day care. Foster home care. Skilled nursing facility. Intermediate care facility.
Cost sharing	Deductible of $150 per person and 25 percent coinsurance, with total cost sharing limited to $1,000 per family but eliminated or reduced for low-income families.	Same as in present Medicare program, but eliminated or reduced for low-income families.	None required, except that the amount of any social security or SSI cash benefits payable would be reduced for persons receiving institutional services.
Administration	Administered by an independent SSA (no longer part of the U.S. Department of Health, Education, and Welfare) in a manner similar to the present Medicare program, using insurance car-		New community centers would provide or arrange for services; supervised by a state

Table 5-12. (*Continued*)

Item	Provisions		
	National health insurance	*Medicare, regular*	*Medicare, long-term benefits*
	riers to process claims (but with new standards for carriers).		agency, with SSA having final authority.
Relationship to other government programs	*Medicare:* revised program would continue, as indicated. *Medicaid:* abolished. *Other programs:* most not affected.		
Financing	*Tax rates:* special tax on payroll (3 percent for employers and 1 percent for employees), 2.5 percent for self-employment and unearned income, and AFDC and SSI payments (3 percent for government and 1 percent for recipients). *Income subject to tax:* first $20,000 annually for combined taxable income of husband and wife or of individual; for an employer, tax on the wages of one employee. *Employment subject to tax:* workers under social security and federal, state, and local employees.	Continuation of same financing provisions.	Enrollees pay premium of $6 per month. Balance to be financed from federal (90 percent) and state (10 percent) general revenues.
Standards for providers of services	Standards similar to Medicare, with additional standards for physicians' assistants. Major surgery and other specialized services covered only when performed by qualified specialists.		Standards for community centers would be established by state agency.
Reimbursement of providers of services	*Institutions:* reimbursed according to prospective reimbursement methods to be developed by SSA. Paid as "participating" providers (see below). *Practitioners:* a fee schedule would be proposed		Community centers reimbursed by state agency according to prospective reimbursement method ap-

Table 5-12. (*Continued*)

Item	Provisions		
	National health insurance	*Medicare, regular*	*Medicare, long-term benefits*
	by a medical society or equivalent organization and approved by SSA. Practitioners who elect to "participate" would receive the scheduled amount, including the cost sharing due from the patient. Nonparticipating practitioners could charge more than the schedule allows, but would have to collect the cost sharing and extra amount from the patient.		proved by SSA.
Delivery and resources	*Regulation of providers:* services, facilities, and capital expenditures of institutions must be approved by state and local planning agencies. *Professional Standards Review Organization:* would apply to all inpatient and outpatient services under the program. *Private insurance:* DHEW would officially certify supplemental private insurance policies meeting specified requirements. *Health resources development board:* would receive 1 percent of national health insurance program funds to improve health resources and delivery; could make grants and loans for development and construction of health maintenance organizations, primary care centers, and certain other organizations, and for specified manpower training; would promote area and state health planning.		

Source: Same as Table 5-4, p. 16.

Table 5-13. Major Features of the Health Security Plan Supported by the AFL-CIO (Kennedy-Griffiths Bill), 1974

Item	Provisions
General concept and approach	A program providing broad benefits, administered by the federal government and financed by payroll taxes and federal general revenues.
Coverage of the population	All U.S. residents.
Benefit structure	No limits on benefits, except as noted below, and no cost sharing. *Institutional services:* hospital; skilled nursing facility up to 120 days per year. *Personal services:* physicians; dentists for children under fifteen (to be extended to age twenty-five, eventually to entire population); home health care; services of other health professionals; laboratory and X-ray. *Other services and supplies:* medical appliances and ambulance; optometrists and eyeglasses; prescription drugs for chronic illnesses and other specified diseases.
Administration	Federal government: administered by a special board in the U.S. Department of Health, Education, and Welfare, with regional and local offices operating the program.
Relationship to other government programs	*Medicare:* abolished. *Medicaid and related programs:* would not pay for services covered under these programs. *Other programs:* most not affected.
Financing	Tax on payroll, self-employed, and unearned income, and federal general revenues. *Tax rates:* 1.0 percent on employee wages and unearned income; 3.5 percent for employers; 2.5 percent for self-employment income; federal general revenues equal to total receipts from taxes. *Income subject to tax:* first $15,000 annually for individuals; total payroll for employers. *Employment subject to tax:* workers under social security and federal, state, and local government employees. State and local governments would not pay employer tax.
Standards for providers of services	Same as under Medicare, but with additional requirements. Hospitals could refuse staff privileges to qualified physicians. Skilled nursing facilities must be affiliated with a hospital, which would take responsibility for the quality of medical services provided. Physicians must meet national standards; major surgery to be performed only by qualified specialists. For all providers: records would be subject to review by regional offices; they could be directed to add or reduce services, provide services in a new location, and establish links with other providers.

Table 5-13. (*Continued*)

Item	Provisions
Reimbursement of providers of services	A national health budget would be established and funds allocated, by type of medical service, to regions and local areas. *Hospitals and nursing homes:* would receive an annual predetermined budget, based on reasonable cost. *Physicians and other professionals:* alternative methods of reimbursement are fee-for-service based on fee schedule, per capita payment for persons enrolled, and (by agreement) full- or part-time salary. Payments for fee-for-service may be reduced if they exceed estimates. *Health maintenance organizations and medical society foundations:* per capita payment for all services (or budget for institutional services). Could retain all or part of savings.
Delivery and resources	*Health planning:* HEW responsible for health planning, in cooperation with state planning agencies. Priority to be given to development of comprehensive care of ambulatory patients. *Health resources development fund:* would ultimately receive 5 percent of total income of program, to be used for improving delivery of health care and increasing health resources. *Health maintenance organizations:* would receive grants for development, loans for construction, and payment to offset operating deficits. *Manpower training:* provision for grants to schools and allowances to students for training physicians for general practice, undermanned specialties, and other health occupations, and for the development of new kinds of health personnel.

Source: Same as Table 5-4, p. 14.

chapter six Cost of National Health Insurance

Predicting the cost of any national health insurance plan is a precarious venture. Accurate estimates require predictions of the number of persons to be covered, the quantity of various medical services demanded and received, the level of reimbursement of providers of services, and the amount of administrative costs. Miscalculations on any of these dimensions can lead to serious under- or overestimates of costs. The task is further complicated by the proposed expansion of insurance coverage to many medical services—such as eye, ear, dental, drug, mental health, family planning, and maternity services—for which there is little current actuarial experience in private health insurance plans and little economic research on the sensitivity of consumer demand to reductions in net price.

Even if the cost of national health insurance could be accurately estimated, how "cost" is defined affects comparisons among plans. For instance, costs could be defined as resource costs—that is, the total amount spent on health care services in the United States whether paid for by the national health insurance plan or not.[1] Alternatively, costs could be defined as expenditures under the plan, excluding any services not covered by the plan, any direct patient payments, and any supplementary insurance coverage not required by the plan. Or, if it is the effect on government budgets that is of primary interest, costs could refer to expenditures by the federal and state governments that would be required by the plan. Finally, any of these concepts of costs could be viewed incrementally—that is, the additional costs over and above amounts that would be spent in the absence of national health insurance.

1. Some providers of medical services, such as physicians, may receive higher compensation than their opportunity cost in other areas of employment because of their monopoly position, limited consumer information, and so forth. Personal health expenditures would then overstate true resource costs.

HEW Cost Study

A 1974 study by the U.S. Department of Health, Education, and Welfare (HEW) permits a comparison of each of the major national health insurance plans along any of these cost dimensions.[2] This study applies a uniform methodology to all plans to derive estimates of costs by sources of payments. All plans are assumed to be in operation throughout 1975, regardless of the actual date of planned implementation, in order to facilitate comparison.

One basic assumption underlying the HEW cost estimates is that a 1 percent decrease in the coinsurance rate will lead to an 0.2 percent increase in the quantity of services consumed.[3] This assumption is somewhat arbitrary, particularly since it does not vary by the magnitude of the change in coinsurance rate involved, or by the distribution of direct payments among individuals. A reduction in coinsurance for a service that is already extensively covered may cause much less response in usage than one for a service that is currently not well covered. Similarly, a change that involves large reductions for some people and none for others may have quite different effects from one that reduces coinsurance rates equally for everyone.

Despite these reservations, the underlying demand assumption can probably be considered a useful starting point for preliminary analysis and to fall within the range of plausible values. Higher or lower magnitudes of the demand response would not change the relative ranking of any of the plans, although it would affect the magnitude of incremental costs for a plan.[4] More refined methods would require additional empirical evidence, perhaps from a national health insurance experiment such as that currently under way at the Rand Corporation,[5] and a more complex model of consumer behavior.

2. U.S. Department of Health, Education, and Welfare, *Estimated Health Expenditures under Selected National Health Insurance Bills,* A Report to the Congress (1974).
3. More precisely, the study assumed that for each additional dollar of medical expenses paid by third parties, total medical expenditures would increase by fifty cents. This relationship was assumed for hospital, physician, and other medical expenditures. An even greater increase was assumed for dental care, family planning services, and long-term care.
4. The selected value of demand elasticity is at the low end of the range of values estimated in a number of econometric studies. See, for example, the studies cited in note 2, p. 62, above.
5. For a description of the experiment, see Joseph P. Newhouse, "A Design for a Health Insurance Experiment," *Inquiry,* vol. 11 (March 1974), pp. 5–7.

A more serious qualification of the HEW study is that the price controls proposed under Phase IV of the 1971–74 Economic Stabilization Program are assumed to be in effect regardless of the provisions of a bill for controls on prices. This means that proposals whose cost controls are not as strong as those of Phase IV are shown to be relatively less expensive than they would actually be. A recent simulation study by Feldstein and Friedman indicates that the cost of national health insurance is quite sensitive to the extent of direct payments by patients and to the supply response of physicians and hospitals.[6] Methods of reimbursing providers that permit no constraints on prices paid, such as that of the American Medical Association, could reasonably be expected to lead to much higher prices than those that would attempt to moderate price increases through more stringent methods of reimbursement.

One aspect of costs that is not thoroughly treated by the HEW study is the indirect cost of national health insurance resulting from current tax provisions. The study estimates any additional tax subsidies that would result from changes in the tax law, but does not attempt to estimate additional tax revenues that would be forgone through greater deductions and subsidies under current tax law. Since many plans would markedly increase premium payments to private health insurance plans, additional forgone tax revenues under some plans could result in a loss of federal tax revenues of billions of dollars, while others, such as the Kennedy-Mills bill, would reduce private insurance premiums and increase tax revenues by several billion dollars.

The HEW study does not indicate the methodology used to estimate the number of people who would be covered under any of the plans.[7] Since most plans involve some element of voluntarism, on the part either of employees or both employers and employees, many people nominally eligible for coverage may not be covered. Nor does the study indicate what assumptions were made to estimate the extent of supplementary private insurance coverage. The extent of supplementary insurance should be sensitive to the tax treatment of its purchase, the extent of direct payments by patients not covered by the national health insurance plan, and

6. Martin Feldstein and Bernard Friedman, "The Effect of National Health Insurance on the Price and Quantity of Medical Care," in Richard N. Rosett (ed.), *The Role of Health Insurance in the Health Services Sector,* A Conference of the Universities–National Bureau Committee for Economic Research (National Bureau of Economic Research, 1975).

7. Presumably, estimates are based on census counts of persons by age and occupation. Estimates of people in poor health would also be required to determine how many people would fall under the subsidized plans.

the responsibilities of employers to purchase the "standard" plan coverage. The HEW study would be of greater value as a basis for more refined estimates if all such underlying assumptions were made explicit.

Given the current state of knowledge, however, any set of underlying assumptions must of necessity be somewhat arbitrary. The HEW study is valuable in that it presumably applies a consistent methodology based on current national health expenditures to the specific provisions of each of the major national health insurance bills. The following sections, therefore, draw upon the HEW study, as well as additional evidence on the extent of tax subsidies and the distribution of costs among income classes.

Resource Costs

The first question to be asked about any national health insurance plan is how it will affect the total production of medical care goods and services. A plan that increases the total cost of personal health care may well be preferred to one that does not, since one of the purposes of national health insurance is to increase the amount of medical care received, particularly by low-income families and those who now lack adequate preventive services. As shown in Table 6-1, total personal health care expenditures are estimated by HEW to increase from $103 billion in 1975 without national health insurance to $107 billion under the Long-Ribicoff plan and to $116 billion under the Health Security Act. Incremental resource costs under the Kennedy-Mills plan are $9.3 billion, compared with $6.5 billion under the administration's plan. Since the Kennedy-Mills and administration plans have similar benefits for middle- and upper-income families, the greater resources available for medical care under the Kennedy-Mills plan largely reflect greater use of medical services by the poor and by lower-income working families.

National Health Insurance Expenditures

The most common meaning of the cost of national health insurance is the amount spent by the plan. This concept of cost excludes amounts for which patients are responsible or expenditures for medical care provided by other public programs. As Table 6-1 shows, expenditures for national health insurance, including any remaining parts of the Medicare and Medicaid plan, would range from $38 billion under the Long-Ribicoff bill to $95 billion under the Health Security Act. This discrepancy exists primarily because the Health Security Act provides a broad range of services free of charge, while the Long-Ribicoff plan assumes responsibility for medical expenses only after the patient has incurred substantial costs. The total costs of the administration and the Kennedy-Mills plans are virtually identical under this concept of cost—$74 and $72 billion, respectively. This is to be expected given the similarity of benefit coverage. The bill sponsored by the Health Insurance Association of America would have a similar cost, but benefits of this plan are concentrated on a smaller segment of the population (it excludes 25 million people from coverage, as compared with 3 million under the Kennedy-Mills bill and 6.5 million under the administration bill). The average cost per person eligible for services is higher under the HIAA bill.

Federal Expenditures

As discussed earlier, however, the plans differ considerably in the sources of their financing. The Long-Ribicoff and Kennedy-Mills plans and the Health Security Act would rely on public financing, while other approaches involve major financing from privately paid premiums. Federal expenditures average about $30 billion under the American Medical Association, Long-Ribicoff, administration, and HIAA bills; about $64 billion under the Kennedy-Mills bill, and $93 billion under the Health Security Act.

Some of these federal expenditures, however, would replace expenditures that would have been made under the current Medicare and Medicaid programs. In addition, they would reduce the cost of subsidizing the direct provision of services through federal hospitals or such delivery programs as neighborhood health centers. Incremental costs to the federal government, therefore, would be substantially less than the above figures. Table 6-1 shows incremental federal revenues to range from $6 billion under the administration plan to $43 billion under the Kennedy-Mills plan (and $73 billion under the Health Security Act). Additional funds for the administration plan would be drawn from general revenues, without specifically increasing taxes, while the K-M plan would place an additional 4 percent payroll tax on the first $20,000 of earnings and a 2.5 percent tax on self-employment income and unearned income up to a total family income of $20,000. The K-M plan would also require about $8.5 billion of additional federal general revenues.

Table 6-1. Federal, State, and Private Expenditures for Alternative National Health Insurance Plans, Based on Prices and Population Projected for 1975
Billions of dollars

Type of expenditure	No national health insurance plan	Supporter or sponsor of plan						
		American Medical Association	Long-Ribicoff	Administration	American Hospital Association	Health Insurance Association of America	Kennedy-Mills	Health Security Act (AFL-CIO)
Real resource costs[a]	103.0	112.8	107.4	109.5	114.0	111.0	112.3	116.0
Incremental expenditures[b]	...	9.8	4.4	6.5	11.0	8.0	9.3	13.0
Expenditures under plan, total[c]	28.1	80.1	37.8	68.6	90.8	74.0	71.5	95.1
Federal	20.1	29.7	28.9	28.2	40.0	30.9	63.5	93.2
State	6.3	4.1	7.2	7.3	2.2	6.0	4.7	1.9
Private	1.7	46.3	1.7	33.1	48.6	37.1	3.3	0.0
Incremental federal expenditures, total[d]	...	8.1	8.3	5.9	18.2	9.5	42.5	73.1
Programs covered by plan	...	9.6	8.8	8.1	19.9	10.8	43.4	73.1
Other programs	...	-1.5	-0.5	-2.2	-1.7	-1.3	-0.9	0.0
Incremental state expenditures, total[d]	...	-4.7	0.0	-1.0	-7.1	-3.0	-3.7	-7.9
Programs covered by plan	...	-2.2	0.9	1.0	-4.1	-0.3	-1.6	-4.4
Other programs	...	-2.5	-0.9	-2.0	-3.0	-2.7	-2.1	-3.5

Source: U.S. Department of Health, Education, and Welfare, *Estimated Health Expenditures under Selected National Health Insurance Bills, A Report to the Congress* (1974) pp. 25, 33, 41, 48, 61, 69, 75. See the discussion in the text for further explanation of the expenditures.

a. Total amount spent on medical care in the United States under the plan.

b. Expenditures in addition to those under the insurance plan. The price of medical care is assumed to be the same regardless of which, if any, plan is implemented. Differences in expenditures among plans, therefore, reflect differences in medical services received.

c. Includes Medicare and Medicaid, when retained in the plan. Excludes supplementary private insurance expenditures, direct payments, and public expenditures not under the plan, which are included in the first row totals in the table.

d. Actual additional cost to the government, as some of the expenditures in the second panel of the table would replace expenditures that would have been made under the current Medicare, Medicaid, and other programs.

Federal Tax Subsidies

The total incremental cost to the federal government, however, depends not only on the amounts to be expended but also on any changes in tax revenues received. The plans sponsored by the American Medical Association, the American Hospital Association, and the Health Insurance Association of America all change the tax laws to permit full deduction of private health insurance premiums from the personal income tax (rather than one-half of the premium up to $150, as under current law). The AMA plan would also permit workers to deduct 80 percent of their employers' contributions to a "standard" plan as if they had been made by the worker directly.

Other plans would not change the current tax treatment of health insurance premiums and medical expenses, but the amount of the tax subsidy would be changed as the extent of private health insurance and direct medical payments was altered. Plans that substantially increase contributions by employers to private health insurance plans, such as the AMA, administration employee, and AHA plans, would result in greater forgone tax revenues as a larger share of workers' incomes took the form of nontaxable fringe benefits.

Table 6-2 presents estimates of the extent of tax subsidies and incremental federal cost of each of the plans. Tax subsidies would range from $8.9 billion in the AHA plan to $1.1 billion in the Health Security Act. The administration's plan would result in some small increases in tax subsidies, while the Kennedy-Mills plan would reduce tax subsidies by $3.5 billion.[8]

8. Tax subsidies are estimated by a simple adjustment of the current subsidies for changes in employer and employee premium payments and the direct medical expenses paid by individuals. Specifically, tax subsidies under any plan are calculated as follows.

Total tax subsidies, TS, are the sum of tax subsidies from employer contributions to health insurance premiums, $TSEMP$, tax subsidies from the deduction of individual health insurance premiums under current tax law, $TSHI$, tax subsidies from the deduction of direct patient payments, $TSPP$, additional tax subsidies from changes in the tax law that are authorized by the insurance plan, $TSCHG$, and tax credits, $TSCRED$. Thus,

$$TS \equiv \frac{TSEMP_0}{EMPPREM_0} \cdot EMPPREM_i = 0.172 \times EMPPREM_i,$$

where $EMPPREM_i$ equals employer premium contributions under plan i. The ratio used for tax subsidies from employer contributions, 0.172, is based on the subsidies of $3.0 billion in 1974 attributable to employer contributions (Edward R. Fried and others, *Setting National Priorities: The 1974 Budget* [Brookings Institution, 1973],

Table 6-2. Federal Tax Subsidies under Alternative National Health Insurance Plans, 1975

Billions of dollars

				Supporter or sponsor of plan				
Source of subsidy	No national health insurance plan	American Medical Association	Long-Ribicoff	Administration	American Hospital Association	Health Insurance Association of America	Kennedy-Mills	Health Security Act (AFL-CIO)
Employer premium contributions	3.4	5.7	3.2	4.5	6.1	4.3	1.1	0.5
Personal income tax deductions								
Under current tax law	2.7	2.4	2.6	2.2	1.8	2.4	1.6	0.6
With changes in law under the plan	...	7.8	...	...	1.0	1.2	...	...
Tax credits	...	14.0	...	...	...	...	...	...
Total federal tax subsidies	6.1	29.9	5.8	6.8	8.9	7.9	2.7	1.1

Source: Estimated as described in note 8 on page 135. Figures are rounded.

Combining changes in federal tax subsidies with incremental federal expenditures provides the total impact on the federal budget of the various health insurance plans. As shown in Table 6-3, federal costs would increase by $6.3 billion under the administration plan, and $39 billion under

---

p. 119, note 7), and 1974 employer contributions of $17.4 billion (HEW, *Estimated Health Expenditures*, p. 3 [average of 1973 and 1975 figures])—3.0/17.4 = 0.172.

A study by Mitchell and Phelps estimates more substantial tax subsidies for employer contributions—25 cents for each dollar of employer premium contributions (Bridger M. Mitchell and Charles E. Phelps, "Employer-Paid Group Health Insurance and the Costs of Mandated National Coverage" [Rand Corporation, 1974; processed], p. 16). If this figure is accurate, changes in federal tax subsidies are underestimated here for those plans that increase employer contributions and overestimated for those plans that reduce them (such as the Kennedy-Mills plan and the Health Security Act).

Tax subsidies from the deduction of health insurance premiums under current tax law are assumed to constitute the same fraction of total individual or employee health insurance premiums as they would in the absence of a national health insurance plan—about 7 cents for every dollar of individual health insurance premiums. So,

$$TSHI \equiv \frac{TSHI_0}{INDPREM_0} \cdot INDPREM_i = 0.070 \times INDPREM_i,$$

where $INDPREM_i$ equals individual premium contributions under plan i. The ratio used for tax subsidies from individual health insurance premiums, $0.8/11.5 = 0.070$, is based on $0.8 billion for 1974 (6/19 of $2.6 billion in total tax subsidies for medical expenses, estimated in *Setting National Priorities: The 1974 Budget*, p. 120). (The proportion is from Bridger M. Mitchell and Ronald J. Vogel, *Health and Taxes: An Assessment of the Medical Deduction*, R-1222-OEO [Rand Corporation, 1973].) Individual health insurance payments in 1974 were $11.5 billion (*Estimated Health Expenditures*, p. 3 [average of 1973 and 1975 figures]).

Similarly, tax subsidies from direct patient payments are assumed to bear the same relationship as tax subsidies to direct patient payments do currently:

$$TSPP \equiv \frac{TSPP_0}{PATPAY_0} \cdot PATPAY_i = 0.062 \times PATPAY_i,$$

where $PATPAY_i$ equals direct patient payments under plan i. The ratio used for tax subsidies from direct patient payments, $1.8/29.1 = 0.062$, is based on the ratio in 1974—3/19 of $2.6 billion (as explained above) or $1.8 billion, and direct patient payments, estimated at $29.1 billion (*Estimated Health Expenditures*, p. 3 [average of 1973 and 1975 figures]).

The assumption that tax subsidies from direct patient payments bear the same relation as those to direct patient payments may be particularly invalid for those plans that would reduce all large medical expenditures, thus reducing the number of families with direct medical expenses in excess of 3 percent of adjusted gross income. However, even in plans with ceilings on family contributions, excluded services such as mental health benefits, extensive dental work, or nursing-home care may allow many families to continue to benefit from the tax deduction for direct medical expenses.

Tax subsidies resulting from changes in the tax law or from tax credits are taken from the HEW cost study, as are employer contributions, individual health insurance premium payments, and direct patient payments under alternative plans.

Table 6-3. Increases in Federal Costs under Alternative National Health Insurance Plans, by Source of Increase, 1975
Billions of dollars

Source of increase	Supporter or sponsor of plan						
	American Medical Association	Long-Ribicoff	Administration	American Hospital Association	Health Insurance Association of America	Kennedy-Mills	Health Security Act (AFL-CIO)
New resources[a]	9.8	4.4	6.5	11.0	8.0	9.3	13.0
Net transfer of current outlays from private to public funding	3.3	3.5	−1.2	2.8	0.2	26.0	47.1
Net transfer from state to federal funding	4.7	0.0	1.0	7.1	3.0	3.7	7.9
Total increase in federal cost[b]	17.8	7.9	6.3	20.9	11.2	39.0	68.0

Source: Same as Table 6-1.
a. From Table 6-1, line 2.
b. Includes effect of changes in existing tax subsidies.

the Kennedy-Mills plan. The federal cost of the AMA plan is more than doubled by including the extent of forgone tax revenues—from $8.1 billion in incremental federal expenditures (which includes the federal tax credits) to $17.8 billion including all tax subsidies.

Table 6-3 also shows that different plans cause quite different shifts in the distribution of costs among private, state, and federal sources. All the administration plan's additional federal costs would go for new resource costs, rather than substituting for state and private expenditures. Under the Kennedy-Mills bill, the federal government would assume financial responsibility for $26 billion of medical expenditures currently borne by the private sector.

State Expenditures

States would continue to assume some responsibility for medical care under most plans. As shown in Table 6-1, state governments would be required to pay $2 billion under the AHA plan and the Health Security Act, and over $7 billion under the administration and Long-Ribicoff plans. These costs would be substantially offset, however, by the decline in Medicaid payments and the reduction in losses or bad debts in government-run charity hospitals. On balance, most states would experience a reduction in total expenditures. HEW estimates that the Long-Ribicoff bill would not change the financial position of state governments, the administration plan would reduce state expenditures for medical care by $1 billion, and the Kennedy-Mills plan would reduce expenditures by $4 billion. Other plans, such as the AHA plan and the Health Security Act, would eliminate most state payments for medical care, resulting in windfall gains of over $7 billion.

Some plans could affect the mix of financial responsibility for medical expenses between state and local governments. Under the administration plan, state expenditures for national health insurance would exceed replaced Medicaid expenditures in every state except Maryland (see Table 6-4). In about half the states, these increases in costs would be offset by reductions in bad debts and losses from charity hospitals, which are run for the most part by cities, counties, or local hospital districts. Southern states would experience quite substantial reductions in charity hospital losses, since many poor people not currently covered by Medicaid would be covered by national health insurance. State expenditures under the plan, however, would be considerably higher than under the Medicaid

Table 6-4. Estimates of State Expenditures and Offsets under the Administration Plan for National Health Insurance, Fiscal Year 1975

Millions of dollars

Region and state	State expenditures			Offsets to expenditures		Net change in state expenditures
	AHCIP	Other[a]	Total	Current Medicaid[b] and general assistance expenditures	Assumed savings for direct hospital expenditures	
United States	4,204.9	2,604.3	6,809.2	5,806.2	2,041.4[c]	−1,038.4[c]
Northeast	1,397.2	1,179.8	2,577.0	2,450.0	743.4	−616.4
Maine	11.8	7.8	19.6	16.2	0.1	3.3
New Hampshire	8.6	6.1	14.7	10.6	0.2	3.9
Vermont	7.9	6.6	14.5	11.3	0.1	3.1
Massachusetts	155.3	141.9	297.2	266.9	32.5	−2.2
Rhode Island	25.3	11.0	36.3	30.3	1.5	4.5
Connecticut	46.3	41.8	88.1	68.2	8.6	11.3
New York	806.2	712.3	1,518.5	1,504.5	586.1	−572.1
New Jersey	146.8	84.4	231.2	208.2	53.3	−30.3
Pennsylvania	189.0	167.9	356.9	333.8	61.0	−37.9
North Central	1,057.4	598.0	1,655.4	1,317.2	362.5[c]	−24.3[c]
Ohio	154.4	67.4	221.8	168.7	63.5	−10.4
Indiana	62.4	38.6	101.0	72.3	26.4	2.3
Illinois	271.0	129.2	400.2	338.9	84.0	−22.7
Michigan	237.0	136.6	373.6	323.1	38.8	11.7
Wisconsin	77.7	73.3	151.0	121.4	5.1	24.5
Minnesota	87.7	67.1	154.8	121.9	34.3	−1.4
Iowa	32.4	20.2	52.6	34.0	13.1	5.5
Missouri	58.9	20.2	79.1	48.8	55.8	−25.5
North Dakota	7.5	4.3	11.8	7.0	0.7	4.1
South Dakota	7.9	4.9	12.8	7.3	n.a.	5.5[c]
Nebraska	20.4	14.9	35.3	24.7	15.0	−4.4
Kansas	40.1	21.3	61.4	49.1	25.8	−13.5
South	919.2	414.7	1,333.9	960.4	707.6	−334.1
Delaware	10.4	4.0	14.4	11.1	8.7	−5.4

Maryland	84.8	34.6	119.4	128.7	38.0	−47.3
District of Columbia	41.8	13.1	54.9	42.5	47.3	−34.9
Virginia	67.8	31.1	98.9	72.8	27.4	−1.3
West Virginia	18.9	4.3	23.2	13.7	0.9	8.6
North Carolina	66.6	25.1	91.7	61.4	29.9	0.4
South Carolina	20.4	8.6	29.0	18.5	8.1	2.4
Georgia	71.0	39.5	110.5	80.8	61.2	−31.5
Florida	103.1	24.6	127.7	78.5	72.2	−23.0
Kentucky	43.4	16.6	60.0	39.3	17.8	2.9
Tennessee	43.5	26.7	70.2	51.5	53.2	−34.5
Alabama	37.7	17.0	54.7	34.8	13.5	6.4
Mississippi	25.3	8.8	34.1	21.7	17.5	−5.1
Arkansas	19.1	11.3	30.4	18.6	7.4	4.4
Louisiana	40.1	20.8	60.9	38.6	108.7	−86.4
Oklahoma	46.5	26.4	72.9	48.2	7.6	17.1
Texas	178.8	102.2	281.0	199.7	188.2	−106.9
West	**831.1**	**411.7**	**1,242.8**	**1,078.6**	**227.9**c	**−63.7**c
Montana	8.3	4.8	13.1	8.1	n.a.	5.0c
Idaho	8.6	3.4	12.0	7.0	0.7	4.3
Wyoming	2.9	1.7	4.6	2.6	3.0	−1.0
Colorado	45.4	26.0	71.4	51.6	29.7	−9.9
New Mexico	12.9	4.3	17.2	9.6	1.8	5.8
Arizona	23.9	0	23.9	…	33.2	−9.3
Utah	8.8	6.5	15.3	9.9	3.5	1.9
Nevada	10.9	4.0	14.9	10.1	n.a.	4.8c
Washington	54.9	38.4	93.3	75.7	19.7	−2.1
Oregon	26.4	16.1	42.5	27.3	22.8	−7.6
California	608.7	294.1	902.8	849.6	105.4	−52.2
Hawaii	15.3	9.7	25.0	23.0	7.8	−5.8
Alaska	4.1	2.7	6.8	4.1	0.3	2.4

Sources: *National Health Insurance*, Hearings before the Senate Committee on Finance, 93 Cong. 2 sess. (1974), pp. 37, 38, 40. Figures are rounded.

n.a. Not available.

a. Residual Medicaid (long-term care), for which the current Medicaid program would be continued, residual general assistance, and expenditures for state-provided services.

b. Includes only offsets for reductions in Medicaid expenditures for services currently covered by Medicaid that would be covered under the administration plan.

c. Does not include hospital expenditures in South Dakota in the North Central region, and Montana and Nevada in the West, which are not available.

program in some states, such as Connecticut, Michigan, Wisconsin, West
Virginia, and Oklahoma. Overall, state expenditures would be more than
$1 billion less than under the current programs.

The Kennedy-Mills plan would reduce expenditures both by state governments and by local governments that run charity hospitals. Expenditures by the states would be set according to 1973 Medicaid expenditure
levels, resulting in $1.6 billion less in state expenditures in 1975 than what
they would be if national health insurance did not replace Medicaid. Bad
debts and losses from charity hospitals would be reduced by an additional
$2.1 billion, with the net result of fiscal relief for many local governments.

Some national health insurance plans would freeze state contributions
at their current levels, while others would require states to increase contributions as the costs of the plan rose. Under the Long-Ribicoff plan,
states would be required to contribute an amount equal to the state's payments under the Medicaid program in the year before enactment (with
additions or subtractions depending on the liberality of the current Medicaid program). State contributions, however, would then remain fixed and
would not increase in future years. Under the Kennedy-Mills plan, states
where the 3 percent tax paid by the state on payments under the Aid to
Families with Dependent Children program was less than Medicaid payments had been would pay an amount equal to the difference. The administration plan would attempt to set state contributions at one-quarter of
the total national health insurance cost after the first year when benefit
data for the assisted plan became available.

Employer Contributions

Any additional costs of national health insurance for employers are
likely eventually to be borne either by consumers, in the form of higher
prices, or by employees, in the form of lower wages.[9] However, in the
short run, employers may incur some windfall gains or losses as these adjustments in the composition of labor costs are gradually made. Furthermore, costs of health insurance may change the relative labor cost of
different kinds of workers. If employers are unable to charge higher prices
for products or to reduce wages for employees (because of minimum

9. See John A. Brittain, *The Payroll Tax for Social Security* (Brookings Institution, 1972), especially chaps. 2 and 3, for an analysis of the incidence of payroll taxes.

wage restrictions), the cost of low-wage workers to employers may be increased, making them relatively less attractive as employees. Temporary, overtime, and part-time workers may then be preferred to full-time workers electing health insurance coverage. Thus, the extent of employer contributions required by a plan can have important labor market effects, unless offset by other public policies.

As shown in Table 6-5, employer contributions to health insurance plans are estimated by HEW to increase from $20 billion in the absence of a national health insurance plan to $27 billion under the administration plan, and to $35 billion under the AHA plan. Employers would be expected to contribute about $7 billion toward supplementary private insurance plans in the Kennedy-Mills plan.[10]

Four plans—the administration, AMA, AHA, and HIAA plans—rely heavily on purchase by employers of standard health insurance plans, that is, a plan that conforms with the provisions of the bill. The HIAA plan would be voluntary for both employers and employees, while the others would require employers to offer standard coverage to workers. The AHA plan requires both full-time and part-time workers to be offered coverage, while the other plans require coverage only for full-time workers. HEW estimates that 116 million people would be enrolled in standard plans under the HIAA bill, compared with 151 million under the AHA plan. Total premiums per family range from $600 under the administration's employee health care plan to $1,010 under the AHA plan. The employer's share of the premium is not specified in the AMA and HIAA plans, but it would be set at a minimum of 75 percent under the administration plan (after three years) and the AHA plan (immediately).

Federal subsidies would mitigate the cost of the plan to employers facing substantial increases in costs under both the administration and the AHA plans. Subsidies under the administration plan would reduce part of the cost for any employer facing more than a 3 percent increase in labor costs. The federal subsidy would be 75 percent of the excess over 3 percent of labor costs, declining by 15 percentage points annually until the subsidy is eliminated after the fifth year. The AHA plan would provide for a federal subsidy equal to the excess of premiums over 4 percent of

10. Employers, however, would be required to pay a 3 percent tax on earnings up to $20,000 under the K-M plan. Employers facing a reduction in health insurance costs because of the plan would be required to pay the employees' share of the payroll tax, provide supplementary insurance, or otherwise compensate employees for the reduction in the employer obligations.

Table 6-5. Employer Contributions and Subsidies, Enrollment, and Premiums for Alternative National Health Insurance Plans, 1975

	Supporter or sponsor of plan							
Description	No national health Insurance	American Medical Association	Long-Ribicoff	Administration	American Hospital Association	Health Insurance Association of America	Kennedy-Mills	Health Security Act (AFL-CIO)
Employer contributions[a] (billions of dollars)	19.9	33.1	18.9	26.6	35.4	24.9	6.6	2.8
Enrollment in plans with employer-employee contributions (millions)	...	140.0	...	137.2	151.2	116.0	...	...
Premium								
Per family (dollars)	...	970	...	600	1,010	920	...	...
Per employee[b] (dollars)	...	644	...	406	667	623	...	...
Employer share of premium	...	Not specified	...	65 percent first 3 years; 75 percent thereafter	75 percent	Not specified; limits placed on premium contributions of low-wage workers	...	...
Employer subsidies	...	Premiums under the plan deductible as business expense; 50 percent of premiums for other plans deductible	...	Subsidy equal to 75 percent of excess of premiums over 3 percent of payroll, declining to zero after 5 years; premiums deductible as business expense	Subsidy equal to excess of premiums over 4 percent of wages, for a maximum of 10 employees; premiums deductible as business expense	Premiums under the plan deductible as business expense; premiums for other plans not deductible after second year	...	

Source: Same as Table 6-1, various pages.
a. Includes contributions to the national health insurance plan and to other insurance plans.
b. Adjusted for families with more than one employee, and workers with a single plan rather than family coverage.

Table 6-6. Mean Annual Premiums for Family Coverage of Full-Time Workers
under Private Health Insurance Plans, and Share Paid by Employers,
by Industry, 1970

Industry	Mean premium		
	Total (dollars)	Amount paid by employer (dollars)	Percent paid by employer
All industries	348	235	68
Agriculture, mining	358	251	70
Construction	347	241	69
Manufacturing	386	312	81
Transportation, communication	333	238	71
Wholesale and retail trade	319	226	71
Finance, insurance, real estate, and business services	344	243	71
Other services	348	181	52

Source: Bridger M. Mitchell and Charles E. Phelps, "Employer-Paid Group Health Insurance and the Costs of Mandated National Coverage" (Rand Corporation, 1974; processed), table 4, p. 10.

wages, for a maximum of ten employees. The subsidy would continue at that same level over time. Under all the proposals calling for an employer plan coverage, employers would be entitled to count contributions toward the standard plan as deductible business expenses. The AMA and HIAA plan would disallow some, or all, of premium contributions to nonstandard plans as legitimate business expenses.

In spite of these provisions, some employers could be expected to incur substantial increases in employee costs initially. Amounts of premiums currently paid by employers are shown in Table 6-6. In 1970, premiums for family health insurance policies paid by employers ranged from $181 in the service industry to $312 in all manufacturing industries; variation among individual firms is undoubtedly even greater. While these amounts are certain to be considerably higher in 1975, most plans would increase employer contributions even more. The administration plan would require all employers to pay $390 per family in the first year. The AHA plan would set the employer contribution at $758 per family. Federal subsidies would not be available after five years in the administration plan, and would be limited to only ten employees in the AHA plan. Thus, many firms that do not currently make significant contributions to health insurance plans would face substantial increases in labor costs.

Table 6-7. Distribution of National Health Insurance Cost to Families, by Income Class, under the Administration and Kennedy-Mills Plans, 1975

Family income class (dollars)	Total cost (billions of dollars)		Percentage distribution		Cost as percent of income	
	Administration	Kennedy-Mills	Administration	Kennedy-Mills	Administration	Kennedy-Mills
All incomes	65.4	69.5	100.0	100.0	6.6	7.0
Under 3,000	4.7	1.8	7.2	2.6	21.9	8.4
3,000–4,999	4.3	2.3	6.6	3.3	14.5	7.8
5,000–9,999	10.7	10.1	16.4	14.5	7.9	7.4
10,000–14,999	13.1	14.0	20.0	20.1	6.8	7.3
15,000–19,999	11.4	14.1	17.4	20.3	6.1	7.5
20,000–24,999	7.7	9.9	11.8	14.2	5.5	7.0
25,000–49,999	9.1	11.5	13.9	16.5	4.8	6.1
50,000 and over	4.4	5.5	6.7	7.9	4.2	5.3

Sources: Author's estimates.

For the administration plan, total revenue (in billions) consists of employee premiums, $26.8; premiums paid by the elderly, $1.7; assisted plan premiums, $4.2; current Medicare revenues, $14.6; federal general revenues, $11.8; and state general revenues, $6.3. The distribution among income classes of employee premiums and Medicare and federal general revenues is based on the Brookings tax file of family units, with incomes projected to calendar year 1975 levels. Premiums from the elderly are distributed on the basis of the money income distribution of elderly families and unrelated individuals in U.S. Bureau of the Census, *Current Population Reports*, Series P-60, no. 93, "Money Income in 1973 of Families and Persons in the United States" (1974), table 6. The state-local proportion of insurance costs is distributed as indicated in Joseph A. Pechman and Benjamin A. Okner, *Who Bears the Tax Burden?* (Brookings Institution, 1974), table 4-10, variant 1c. The assisted plan premiums are distributed by the author's estimate of $2.6 billion to the under–$3,000 income class and $1.6 billion to the $3,000–$4,999 class. Totals exclude Medicaid expenditures for nonplan services (which are included in Table 6-1).

For the Kennedy-Mills plan, total revenue (in billions) consists of new payroll taxes, $31.5; premiums paid by the elderly, $1.7; current Medicare revenues, $14.6; federal general revenues, $17.0; and state general revenues, $4.7. Payroll taxes are distributed on the basis of the Brookings tax file; the other distributions are as for the administration plan.

Figures are rounded.

Cost to Individuals by Income Class

The cost of national health insurance, whether nominally paid by federal or state governments or by employers, must ultimately be borne by individuals. Of primary concern in the analysis of the cost of any national health insurance plan, therefore, is the distribution of that cost among people of different income classes. Of two plans with the same cost, and even the same distribution of benefits, one plan may be preferred because the costs are distributed more equitably among income classes.

Table 6-7 compares the distribution among income classes of the costs of the administration and Kennedy-Mills plans. The costs shown exclude any payments by patients not covered by the plans and any remaining parts of the Medicare and Medicaid programs. Total costs are about $65 to $70 billion under each plan.

Several assumptions are required to allocate all of the costs among individuals of various income classes. Premiums paid by employers under the administration plan are assumed to be borne by the employees on whose behalf the contributions are made. Payroll taxes on both employers and employees are assumed to be borne by employees in proportion to their taxed earnings. Half of the corporation income tax and all of the property tax are regarded as taxes on property income and are distributed in proportion to the property income reported by each household. Half of the corporation income tax is assumed to be borne by stockholders.[11]

The administration plan falls much more heavily on lower-income families than the Kennedy-Mills plan. About 22 percent of the cost is borne by families with incomes below $3,000 under the administration plan, compared with 8 percent under the Kennedy-Mills plan. The administration plan is also more costly for working families with incomes between $3,000 and $10,000. Such families pay $15 billion toward the administration plan, compared with $12 billion required in the Kennedy-Mills plan.

When the costs of the two plans are compared with income, the administration plan is highly regressive over the entire income range. People with family incomes below $3,000 contribute 22 percent of their income to the plan, compared with 4 percent of income for those with incomes

11. For a complete discussion of the theory and rationale for these assumptions, see Joseph A. Pechman and Benjamin A. Okner, *Who Bears the Tax Burden?* (Brookings Institution, 1974). The assumptions made here correspond to variant 1c, discussed on p. 38 of their book.

Table 6-8. Payments Made by Patients under the Administration and Kennedy-Mills National Health Insurance Plans, with Alternative Family Medical Expenses, by Selected Family Incomes, 1975

| Family income (dollars) | $1,000 annual medical bills[a] | | | | $5,000 annual medical bills[b] | | | |
| | Amount (dollars) | | Percent of income | | Amount (dollars) | | Percent of income | |
	Administration	Kennedy-Mills	Administration	Kennedy-Mills	Administration	Kennedy-Mills	Administration	Kennedy-Mills
2,000	100	0	5.0	0.0	120	0	6.0	0.0
4,000	278	0	7.0	0.0	360	0	9.0	0.0
6,000[c]	400	300	6.7	5.0	720	300	12.0	5.0
8,000	513	475	6.4	5.9	1,500	800	18.8	10.0
10,000	513	475	5.1	4.8	1,500	1,000	15.0	10.0
20,000	513	475	2.6	2.4	1,500	1,000	7.5	5.0

Sources: Calculated by author from provisions of H.R. 12684 and H.R. 13870, introduced in the Ninety-third Congress.
a. Assumes four family members with expenses (excluding drugs and preventive services) of $750, $150, $50, and $50.
b. Assumes four family members with expenses (excluding drugs and preventive services) of $650, $150, $150, and $50.
c. For the administration plan, assumes coverage under the assisted portion (but excludes premium of $300).

Figure 6-1. Typical Cost of National Health Insurance as a Percentage of Family Income under the Administration and Kennedy-Mills Plans, 1975

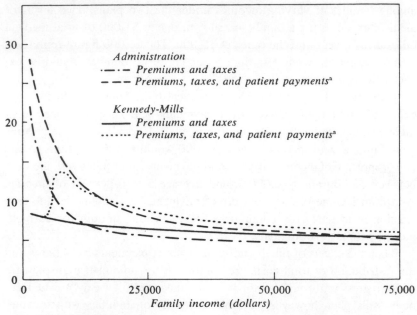

Percent of income

Sources: Same as Table 6-8.
a. Assumes annual medical expenditures $1,000, which represents an average experience.

above $50,000. The cost of the Kennedy-Mills plan is distributed approximately in proportion to income, with the lowest-income and middle-income groups paying 7 to 8 percent of their income and the highest-income group paying 5 percent.

While both the administration and Kennedy-Mills bills derive some revenues from federal and state general revenues, what distinguishes their sources of financing is the heavy reliance on premiums in the administration plan compared with a payroll tax on the first $20,000 of earnings in the Kennedy-Mills plan. This difference is reflected in the declining proportion of income devoted to national health insurance in the administration plan and the constant proportion of income (up to the $20,000 level) applied to the Kennedy-Mills health insurance plan.

In addition to contributing to national health insurance through taxes and premiums, individuals would be required to meet some of their own medical expenses directly under most plans. The administration and Kennedy-Mills plans would require substantial direct patient payments for higher-income families, but payments for lower-income patients would be reduced in the administration plan and eliminated in the Kennedy-Mills plan. Table 6-8 summarizes the distribution of direct patient payments among families of varying incomes under the two plans. Two levels of medical expenses for a family are shown, one at $1,000 of total medical bills during a year and the other at $5,000. The $1,000 figure represents average expenses, while less than 5 percent of all families would be expected to incur expenses above $5,000.

In the typical case of $1,000 in medical bills, families with incomes below $10,000 would make direct payments of from 5 to 7 percent of their incomes under the administration plan. Under the Kennedy-Mills plan, families with incomes below $5,000 would not be required to pay any proportion of income directly, and payments for families with incomes between $5,000 and $10,000 would average 5 to 6 percent of income. Above an income of $10,000, direct payments by patients decline as a fraction of income (by remaining a fixed constant amount for all high-income people) in both plans.

When the effects of the distribution of direct payments by patients and the distribution of total costs are combined, the administration plan remains regressive throughout the income range (see Figure 6-1). The Kennedy-Mills plan, however, falls more heavily on families with incomes between $5,000 and $20,000 than on either lower- or higher-income families.

chapter seven **Benefits and Consequences**
of National Health Insurance

Since any of the proposed national health insurance plans promises to be costly, it is important to review the benefits that can be expected. Just as in defining an appropriate measure of the cost, there are alternative ways of assessing the benefits of a health insurance program. One approach might be to examine the impact of a new system of financing health care on the general health of the American people and to assess the effects of this improved health on greater productivity and well-being. Another approach would be to estimate the value of reduced concern over the possibility of incurring severe financial hardship in meeting medical bills. Still another approach would be to examine the distribution of medical payments, in effect equating receipt of medical services with the benefits of the plan.

While there is merit in all of these approaches, the evaluation of the benefits that can be expected from any health insurance plan is perhaps best undertaken in terms of the original goals. These goals are to ensure that everyone has access to medical care, that no one faces financial hardship as a result of large medical bills, and that incentives are created for limiting the rise in health care costs. The following sections examine the likely success of each of the major plans in meeting these goals.

Impact on the Poor

The first major goal of national health insurance is to ensure that everyone has access to high-quality medical care. Experience with the Medicaid program has demonstrated that adequate financing can increase the utilization of medical services by the poor to levels commensurate with those of higher-income groups. However, if providers of medical services are

penalized with lower financial compensation for treating the poor instead
of other patients, the supply of high-quality medical care easily and con-
veniently accessible to the poor will be restricted. Thus, it is important to
explore not only which medical services a plan puts financially within the
means of the poor but also the ability and willingness of medical care providers to supply the poor with high-quality services.

With the exception of the Health Security Act, which provides comprehensive health services free of charge to all, the major health insurance
proposals all contain special provisions subsidizing the care of the poor
more heavily than others. For this purpose, income is defined in the trade
association plans (American Medical Association, American Hospital
Association, and Health Insurance Association of America) as taxable
adjusted gross income; the administration, Kennedy-Mills, and Long-
Ribicoff bills propose a broader definition of income, including transfer
payments and income from a wide variety of sources. Eligibility income
limits for full benefits average about $5,000 for a family. In addition, par-
tial benefits are extended to families with incomes of up to $8,000 or
$10,000 under all but the Long-Ribicoff bill, which limits partial benefits
to those with incomes that have been reduced to $4,800 or below when
medical expenses are deducted.

As shown in Table 7-1, about 45 to 50 million low-income people
would receive some subsidies for medical care under most bills.[1] An additional 22 to 24 million of the elderly and disabled would be covered under
a special plan for the elderly or under a Medicare program. Total expenditures for low-income persons would be lowest under the Long-Ribicoff
plan (which tapers off benefits rapidly as income rises) and the AMA
plan (which provides a limited range of benefits).

All the plans represent a major improvement over the Medicaid program by covering nearly all those with low incomes. None of the proposals
would exclude families or individuals from coverage on the basis of geographical location, family size, employment status, or welfare status. In
some of the plans a small number of low-income people may fail to be
covered because they are poor health risks, because they have yet to obtain
a full-time job but are too old for coverage under their parents' policy (as
in the Kennedy-Mills plan), or because they fear they will be refused a

1. The AHA plan would provide subsidies only to those with low incomes who
are ineligible for an employee plan; this would make only 35 million people eligible
for government-subsidized care.

Table 7-1. Subsidies for Low-Income People under Alternative National Health
Insurance Plans, 1975

	Supporter or sponsor of plan					
Item	American Medical Association	Long-Ribicoff	Adminis-tration	American Hospital Association	Health Insurance Association of America	Kennedy-Mills
Number of people receiving subsidies (millions)						
Low-income	49.0	44.1	51.1	35.2	50.0	n.a.
Elderly and disabled	24.2	24.1	22.4	22.5	24.2	24.2
People not covered by plan (millions)	4.0	0.0	6.5	8.3	25.0	3.0
Expenditures (billions of dollars)						
For low-income people	14.0	18.2	25.1	26.0[a]	26.6	27.0[a]
For the elderly and disabled	13.7	13.7	16.7	17.4[a]	13.7	23.7
Income limit for full benefits (dollars)						
Family of four	4,300	4,800	5,000	6,000	4,000	4,800
Single individual	1,000	2,400	3,500	2,000	2,000	2,400
Income limit for partial benefits (dollars)						
Family of four	9,500	4,800 plus medical expenses[b]	7,500	10,500	8,000	8,800
Single individual	7,000	2,400 plus medical expenses[b]	3,250	6,000	4,000	6,400
Income definition	Adjusted gross income	Broad	Broad	Adjusted gross income	Adjusted gross income	Broad

Sources: U.S. Department of Health, Education, and Welfare, *Estimated Health Expenditures under Selected National Health Insurance Bills*, A Report to the Congress (1974); and Saul Waldman, *National Health Insurance Proposals: Provisions of Bills Introduced in the 93rd Congress as of July 1974*, U.S. Social Security Administration, Office of Research and Statistics, DHEW Publication (SSA) 75-11920 (1974), and ibid., *as of February 1974*.
n.a. Not available.
a. Author's estimate.
b. The Long-Ribicoff bill includes a "spend-down" provision that enables families with large medical expenditures to qualify for coverage if their incomes net of medical expenditures are below $4,800.

job if they elect coverage (as could occur in the administration plan).[2]
Closing these gaps and requiring universal coverage would ensure that the
goal of adequate access to medical care for all is attained.

The Long-Ribicoff and Kennedy-Mills plans provide a wide range of
benefits free of charge to all families with incomes below $5,000 (see
Table 7-1 for income limits). The administration plan would require even
the very poor to expend as much as 6 percent of income on direct medical
payments, and families with incomes between $2,500 and $5,000 would
face a maximum ceiling of 9 percent of income. Very low income families
are apt to find the cost-sharing requirements of the administration plan
prohibitive, thus undermining the goal of increased access to medical services for the poor. On the other hand, the complete lack of cost sharing
by families with incomes up to $5,000 in the Long-Ribicoff and Kennedy-

2. Although employers are prohibited from discriminating on this basis, enforcement may be difficult.

Mills bills could lead to wasteful use of medical services by some low-income families.

A further difficulty of the Long-Ribicoff and Kennedy-Mills plans is their abrupt termination of benefits as income rises. In the Long-Ribicoff proposal, benefits are reduced dollar for dollar as income rises above $5,000. In the Kennedy-Mills plan, benefits are reduced somewhat more gradually—by twenty-five cents for each additional dollar of income—but the rise in expenditures is still quite substantial for those just above the poverty level. These abrupt increases in costs can pose significant work disincentives and discourage family members from seeking overtime work or the employment of additional family members. Furthermore, they could engender resentment in those who, by earning slightly more, are penalized heavily through reductions in medical benefits.

The Health Security Act would avoid these pitfalls by providing the same benefits at no direct cost to everyone, regardless of income. While this would eliminate the disincentives created by an abrupt termination of benefits as income rises, it does not guarantee that the poor will receive adequate care. Since care will be free to everyone, not just the poor, the poor will have to compete with others for a limited supply of medical services, and they are at a disadvantage in that high-income families tend to live in areas with a greater concentration of medical resources and many medical care providers have a preference for patients from a similar socioeconomic class. Without a financial advantage, the poor may be unable to overcome their existing disadvantage of more limited physical access to medical care.

To the extent that higher-income families purchase supplementary private insurance to meet the deductible and coinsurance provisions of the administration, Kennedy-Mills, and Long-Ribicoff proposals, the advantage to the poor of lower direct payments by patients will be offset or eliminated. To prevent or minimize such an occurrence, purchase of supplementary insurance should be either prohibited or, at the minimum, tax subsidies that promote its purchase should be eliminated.

Methods of reimbursing providers can also affect the services received by the poor. The Health Security Act discourages providers from accepting low-income patients with a multitude of health problems because of its emphasis on capitation payments. Thus, patients requiring more time and effort will be less attractive to a physician or medical organization than those with fewer medical problems.[3]

3. For an elaboration of this point, see John Holahan, *Financing Health Care for the Poor: The Medicaid Experience* (Lexington Books, 1975), pp. 100–02.

The Kennedy-Mills, administration, and Long-Ribicoff plans also contain provisions that discourage providers from supplying high-quality care to lower-income families. The administration and Long-Ribicoff plans permit physicians to derive greater income from the treatment of nonpoor patients by requiring that care for the poor be provided at an established reimbursement level, while physicians may use their discretion in setting charges for higher-income patients.[4] The Kennedy-Mills plan would permit physicians to charge any patient more than the established fee. While this does not institutionalize two-class treatment, higher-income patients are more likely to be able to offer a greater financial inducement to physicians to provide high-quality care. None of the bills prohibits physicians from discriminating among patients in the amount, type, or quality of care rendered on the basis of income (or any other basis).

Nearly all the major national health insurance bills provide a broad package of benefits to most low-income people at minimal or no direct cost to the patient. Only the administration bill requires substantial payments by patients, of up to 6 or 9 percent of income. Some plans restrict services essential to the poor, such as well-baby care, family planning, and eye and ear care for children. Several plans provide only limited skilled nursing-home care.

With the exception of these limits on benefits or coverage, however, the success of the plans in meeting the goal of ensuring high-quality medical care to those unable to pay depends in large part on the availability of medical resources in low-income communities and on the willingness of providers to provide high-quality services to the poor. Experience with Medicaid and Medicare indicates that members of minority groups and rural residents often encounter special difficulties in obtaining adequate medical care, even with an extensive financing program.

Minorities and Access to Medical Care under National Health Insurance

Benefits from the Medicare and Medicaid programs have been disproportionately low for minorities. Fewer blacks eligible for benefits visit physicians, and those receiving a physician's care are much more likely to receive it from hospital outpatient departments than from family physicians or private specialists. Blacks, even when covered by Medicaid or

---

4. Physicians agreeing to accept the established reimbursement level for all patients receive some billing and collecting advantage, but this is likely to offer little inducement for physicians with already high incomes.

Medicare, receive more of their hospital care from crowded city or county hospitals than do whites. Few elderly blacks manage to receive nursing-home benefits, in spite of their more limited resources in the home for providing needed care.

Hearings of the House Judiciary Committee indicate that this pattern of lower benefits is a reflection of both overt and institutional discriminatory practices.[5] The Medicare program has interpreted the Civil Rights Act as applying to the provision of institutional care but not to services rendered by physicians. Administrators of the program view the physician part of Medicare as involving payments to patients for medical care received, rather than direct payments to physicians; so they have not assumed responsibility for ensuring that care is offered in a nondiscriminatory manner. Physicians can refuse to treat minority patients, maintain segregated waiting rooms, or reserve only limited hours for treatment of minority patients without fear of disqualification as Medicare providers. Such discriminatory practices continue to exist in many communities.[6]

Discriminatory practices by physicians also restrict access of minorities to high-quality hospital and nursing-home care. If blacks are unable to obtain the services of the private physicians who are willing to admit them to private hospitals or nursing homes, the range of institutional alternatives available to blacks is limited. As a consequence, a disproportionate number of blacks covered by medical care financing programs receive care from crowded public hospitals, and few blacks are admitted to nursing homes.

While direct discrimination by hospitals is prohibited in Medicare and Medicaid, considerable disparities among races in the care received continue to exist. Deficiencies in administration of the programs are partly responsible for this failure. Only about 5 percent of medical facilities were site-visited to check for compliance in the fifteen months ending in March 1973, and fewer than 3 percent in 1971.[7] There are no well-established grievance or complaint procedures for patients to bring discriminatory charges against institutions, and many patients are not even aware that they are entitled to care in private hospitals. The Medicare program

5. *Title VI Enforcement in Medicare and Medicaid Programs,* Hearings before the Subcommittee on Civil Rights and Constitutional Rights of the House Committee on the Judiciary, 93 Cong. 1 sess. (1974).

6. See, for example, the speech delivered by Melbah McAfee at the conference, "Resolved: The South Will Feed Its Hungry" (University of North Carolina, June 23, 1974; transcription).

7. *Title VI Enforcement,* Hearings, p. 29.

has not insisted that hospitals and nursing homes have affirmative action programs to attract minority patients. Thus, facilities whose staff physicians do not treat minority patients continue to have only white patients, even in the absence of direct discriminatory practices by the hospital or nursing home.

None of the national health insurance plans would eliminate the shortcomings that have existed in the Medicare and Medicaid programs. None of the plans contains provisions prohibiting physicians from discriminating on the basis of race, creed, or national origin. None establishes administrative procedures for enforcing nondiscriminatory provisions, informing beneficiaries of their rights to high-quality services, or eliciting patient complaints of discriminatory treatment. None of the plans includes positive programs to offset past patterns of discriminatory practices by increasing the availability of physicians willing to practice in minority neighborhoods or promoting the development of organizations providing medical care in these communities. The Kennedy-Mills plan would provide funds for a health resources development board, but these funds are not specifically targeted on the problems of access to medical care faced by minorities.

In the absence of such safeguards, it can be anticipated that the benefits of national health insurance will not be equitably distributed. Instead, the pattern of Medicare and Medicaid, in which whites receive average payments for physicians that are 35 to 60 percent higher than those received by blacks and other minorities, is likely to persist, and the goal of ensuring quality medical care for all Americans will not be fully achieved.

Rural Residents and National Health Insurance

While the introduction of the Medicaid program in 1966 caused the poor as a whole to make rapid gains in the use of medical services, rural residents have not experienced any gains in use relative to urban residents. The failure of Medicaid and Medicare to reach many rural residents suggests that national health insurance, too, may be less than fully successful in rural areas.

Several factors have contributed to the failure of medical care financing programs to reach rural communities. First, and undoubtedly most important, most rural communities have only limited medical resources. A national health insurance plan that covers dental care, home health visits, podiatry services, and skilled nursing-home care is likely to be of little benefit to a rural community without a physician, much less the specialists and facilities required to offer these comprehensive services.

Second, state and federal restrictions on who can provide medical care prevent the optimal use of paramedical personnel. Even though a thoroughly trained nurse practitioner or medex could provide needed medical care in rural communities, state licensing restrictions that require a physician to be physically present when care is rendered limit the usefulness of such personnel. If medical care financing plans will not pay for services rendered by paramedical personnel or make direct payments to primary health centers employing them, innovative uses of such personnel are further hampered.

Third, transportation is frequently an important barrier to medical care in isolated rural communities. Without special programs to bring either patients to medical services or medical services to patients, many rural residents, particularly those with low incomes, are unable to receive care even if it is provided at low or no cost.

Fourth, since the poor in rural areas are inadequately represented by organizations supporting their interests, they are more likely to have a variety of problems that contribute to poor health, such as insufficient income maintenance, poor housing, inadequate diets, impure water, and inadequate sanitation. These conditions intensify the medical care needs of the rural poor, while at the same time limiting the effectiveness of medical care treatment. A child with parasites or inadequate nutrition, for instance, is unlikely to be able to be permanently helped by medical treatment. Coordination of medical care services with other supporting services, therefore, is particularly crucial.

Finally, few forces exist to induce a greater concentration of medical resources in rural communities. Medical schools rarely adequately prepare students for rural practice, and in fact frequently undermine their confidence to provide quality care in an area without specialized supporting services. Those physicians practicing in rural areas frequently resist new entrants to medical practice in the area, recognizing that they can earn an adequate income only by working long hours and providing a large volume of service at a low charge per patient.[8] Medicare and Medicaid have not altered this situation, because they have followed the practice of paying physicians on the basis of prevailing charges. Thus, physicians

8. See *Competition in the Health Services Market,* Hearings before the Subcommittee on Antitrust and Monopoly of the Senate Committee on the Judiciary, 93 Cong. 2 sess. (1974), pt. 2, pp. 599–607; and Jack Anderson, "Medical Monopolies: Another Ailment for the Poor," *Washington Post,* May 12, 1974.

practicing in traditionally low-income communities continue to be under-compensated for the care they provide.

National health insurance alone can not counter all these forces militating against adequate medical care in rural areas. However, through careful design it can avoid some of the problems inherent in Medicare and Medicaid.

Both the administration and Kennedy-Mills plans provide for reimbursement of services rendered by paramedical personnel under the supervision of a physician, but the physician is only required to assume responsibility for the care provided and not to be physically present at the time care is rendered. This should facilitate greater use of supplementary medical personnel in rural areas. Direct payment to primary health centers for such services would further promote their use.

The method of reimbursement of providers under the administration and Kennedy-Mills plans, however, would perpetuate past patterns of charges. Thus, those physicians electing to practice in traditionally under-served areas would continue to be penalized through lower compensation. These problems would be intensified in the administration plan, which leaves establishment of reimbursement levels to state governments. A national reimbursement policy that does not discriminate against rural areas is essential to avoid disincentives for location in rural areas. Paying physicians more for rural practice might be required to correct the imbalance in the distribution of physicians.

A supplementary program to improve the availability of resources in rural communities should be an important part of a national health insurance plan. The health resources development board provided for in the Kennedy-Mills plan would channel funds into the creation of additional medical resources, but these funds are not targeted specifically on rural areas and may largely be spent on medical school training and the development of organizations that do not benefit rural areas.[9]

Special programs designed to meet the particular needs of rural areas should also be pursued to ensure that the goals of national health insurance are achieved. These could take the form of furnishing transportation services in isolated communities; coordinating medical services with other services contributing to the health of the community; training medical personnel willing and suited to practice in rural communities; and encouraging the development of innovative rural health delivery programs.

---

9. The bill gives the board general authority to train and recruit professionals who agree to practice in rural areas.

Table 7-2. Maximum Liability for Out-of-Pocket Medical Expenses for a Family of Four under Alternative National Health Insurance Plans

Annual family income (dollars)	Supporter or sponsor of plan									
	American Medical Association[a]		Administration[b]		American Hospital Association[c]		Health Insurance Association of America		Kennedy-Mills	
	Amount (dollars)	Percent of income	Amount (dollars)	Percent of income	Amount (dollars)	Percent of income	Amount (dollars)	Percent of income	Amount (dollars)	Percent of income
2,000	0	0	120	6	0	0	50	3	0	0
4,000	40	1	360	9	0	0	50	1	0	0
5,000	125	3	600	12	0	0	100	2	50	1
6,000	210	4	720	12	0	0	200	3	300	5
8,000	380	5	1,200	15	500	6	400	5	800	10
10,000	550	6	1,500	15	750	8	1,000	10	1,000	10
20,000	1,500	8	1,500	8	2,000	10	1,000	5	1,000	5

Source: Calculated by author from provisions of bills.

a. Amounts and percentages are based on 10 percent of taxable income (after exemptions and deductibles) and on the assumption that families claim the standard deduction.

b. Assumes coverage under the assisted plan for families with incomes below $10,000. For those covered under an employee plan, the maximum patient liability is $1,500.

c. Based on head of family being under sixty-five. Ceilings for family heads of sixty-five and older are one-half those for younger persons.

Impact on Those with Large Medical Expenses

The second major goal of national health insurance is to protect all families from the financial hardship of large medical expenses. Private health insurance plans have failed to protect everyone from the financial consequences of poor health by excluding some benefits from coverage, by refusing coverage to poor health risks, and by setting limits on the maximum amounts that will be paid. Furthermore, only half the population now has any major medical coverage at all.

All the major national health insurance proposals would reverse the pattern of private health insurance coverage to incorporate the principle of a ceiling on *patient* liability for medical costs. Furthermore, all plans, except for the Long-Ribicoff plan, recognize that what constitutes a catastrophic medical expense depends on family income, and hence vary the ceiling with income.[10] The maximum ceiling for the highest-income families is set at 10 percent of income under the AHA and AMA plans, at $1,000 under the Kennedy-Mills and HIAA plans, and at $1,500 under the administration plan (see Table 7-2 for ceilings for lower-income families). The Health Security Act, of course, provides complete protection against financial hardship by covering virtually all medical costs.

In spite of the desirability of setting ceilings on family contributions, it is still possible under most plans for a family to incur severe financial burdens. First, most plans exclude substantial numbers of people from coverage. This ranges from 3 million people in the Kennedy-Mills plan to 25 million in the HIAA plan (which would provide insurance to "uninsurable" or poor health risk persons only at "actuarially fair," that is, prohibitively expensive, premiums).

Second, some plans do not provide ceilings for all covered persons. The HIAA plan places a ceiling on expenditures for those covered under employee group plans, but not for people who purchase individual coverage. The Long-Ribicoff proposal limits family contributions to the first sixty days of hospital care, the first $2,000 of medical bills, and an additional $1,000. In dollar terms, however, this "ceiling" could be quite high, since very large bills could be incurred in a hospital stay of less than sixty days. The ceiling is also so high as to provide little protection against severe financial burdens for all except the very highest income families. Many

10. The Long-Ribicoff bill would help only those families who spent all but $4,800 of their income on medical care.

families with incomes between, say, $5,000 and $10,000 are unlikely to have private health insurance coverage to meet the sizable deductibles, and hence could incur severe financial hardship in the event of a medical catastrophe.

Third, all plans exclude some medical services from coverage. The Long-Ribicoff proposal does not cover prescription drugs, which can be very costly for patients with chronic illnesses requiring continuous drug therapy. Limitations on nursing-home care are contained in all plans, even the Health Security Act. The Kennedy-Mills plan, however, would introduce a new program to provide long-term care for the elderly. Coverage of dental care is usually either restricted or nonexistent.

Finally, a number of plans permit physicians to charge patients more than the amounts that will be paid by the insurance plan. Thus, a patient undergoing complex surgery might receive a physician's bill several thousand dollars in excess of amounts that would be paid by the plan. Requiring physicians to accept the allowed charge as total payment would help protect everyone from the possibility of excessive financial burden.

Effect of Inflation on Medical Care Costs

The prospects of achieving the third goal of national health insurance —to limit the rise in health care costs—are not as bright under any of the major proposals. All the proposals are expected to result in a net reduction in direct payments by patients for medical care, and hence are likely to contribute to upward pressures on costs. Nonetheless, some characteristics of the major plans would help to constrain costs. All the plans cover lower-cost substitutes for inpatient hospital care, including payment for physician services whether provided in a hospital or on an ambulatory basis. The administration and Kennedy-Mills plans provide optional coverage under approved prepaid health plans, where reimbursement is made to the carrier on a capitation basis; the Health Security Act and the American Hospital Association plan contain specific subsidies or incentives for coverage under such organizations.

Some plans, however, have such extensive insurance coverage even for families reasonably able to meet their medical expenses directly as to invalidate any automatic market incentives for efficiency or cost constraint. The Health Security Act, the American Medical Association plan, and the American Hospital Association plan all contain minimal or no direct patient payments on a wide range of medical services for all income classes. The nominal payments required under the American Hospital Association plan are not related to the cost of care and provide little incentive to choose lower-cost alternatives. The Health Insurance Association of America plan also contains only moderate cost-sharing requirements; however, a substantial fraction of the population (25 million people) would not be covered by the plan so that the only important source of market cost constraint would come from those unfortunate few.

The Long-Ribicoff and Kennedy-Mills plans would require more substantial contributions from middle- and upper-income families but would exempt all low-income families from any contribution to medical care costs. Incorporating some minimal cost sharing for all except the poorest of these families might mitigate against any possible wasteful or inefficient use of medical care. The administration plan requires substantial contributions from everyone, including amounts that are possibly excessive for low-income families. While it can be argued that both the Long-Ribicoff and administration plans require excessive direct patient payments for lower-income working families (particularly those with incomes of $5,000 to $10,000), reasonable direct patient payments for those with higher incomes, such as those required in the Kennedy-Mills plan, could be quite helpful in constraining medical care costs. However, the impact of these provisions would be mitigated by any purchase of supplementary private insurance. The Long-Ribicoff, administration, and Kennedy-Mills plans not only permit the purchase of such coverage, but actually encourage it through tax subsidies and other incentives. Elimination of these provisions is essential if the cost-sharing requirements of the standard plan are to have any significant effect in containing costs. Automatic upward adjustment of patient payments over time as total medical expenditures rise is also essential.

Even under plans retaining substantial payments by patients, however, the increased pressures of demand, particularly for ambulatory services, are likely to lead to substantial price increases unless special measures are taken to contain prices. Thus, the methods of paying physicians and other medical care providers is of the utmost importance. The Health Security Act contains the most stringent cost control measures. Emphasis is placed on capitation and salary reimbursement, even for physicians in solo practice. Radically changing the methods of compensating physicians, however, can lead to rejection of the plan by the providers whose cooperation is essential to its success. Furthermore, a switch from traditional fee-for-service reimbursement can have its own adverse incentives. Physicians could be expected to prefer patients with simpler medical problems, and waiting times and quality of care might degenerate as physicians attempted to constrain the amount of care provided per patient.

At the other end of the spectrum, the American Medical Association plan and the American Hospital Association plan contain generous provisions for the compensation of providers. Payments to physicians would be on the basis of usual and customary charges in the American Medical Association plan, and the government would be specifically prohibited from establishing any cost control measures. The American Hospital Association plan would compensate hospitals and other institutional providers for a wide range of costs, including "price level depreciation" expenses, investment expenses, and research and educational expenses.

The Long-Ribicoff plan would continue the Medicare model of reimbursement, reimbursing hospitals on the basis of reasonable costs and physicians according to a given percent of usual and customary charges. It is unlikely to be much more successful than the Medicare program in restraining costs.

The administration and Kennedy-Mills plans would develop new methods of reimbursing providers. Under the administration plan, states would be given the responsibility for establishing exactly how this would be done. The Kennedy-Mills plan would make available one or more methods of prospective reimbursement (after consultation with interested groups), with the exact method to be selected at the option of the provider. A "quality management" payment of 50 percent of the difference between the hospital's rate of cost increase in a year and the increase in the "class average rate" would be awarded. At least one-half of this quality management payment would be paid to employees and medical staff. While these innovative methods of institutional reimbursement are intriguing, little evidence is yet available on their potential effectiveness.

Physicians would be reimbursed according to a fee schedule under both the administration and Kennedy-Mills plans. While exact procedures for establishing the schedules are not specified in either plan, different fees for different geographical areas are likely to penalize those areas where medical charges have typically been lower and reward those areas where physicians have been able to earn higher incomes. Thus, the method of compensating physicians would freeze the existing set of financial incentives for physician location, with those areas that have been attractive to physicians in the past continuing to be most attractive in the future.

Similarly, compensating services rendered by specialists at a much higher level than services rendered by family physicians would entrench existing incentives for physicians to specialize. Such distortions would contribute to the inefficient allocation of resources and raise the true costs of national health insurance.

Even more importantly, however, these methods of physician reimbursement would not effectively constrain cost increases. Any physician electing to do so may charge patients (other than the poor and elderly under the administration plan) more than the established fee. Physicians electing to accept the established fee receive some billing and collection advantages, but, given the increased demand likely to be generated, most physicians are likely to opt for the more generous incomes they can derive from setting their own fees.

Finally, even if fees are constrained, expenditures on physician services may rise precipitously as physicians proliferate the number of services provided, increasingly request follow-up visits, charge for telephone calls and miscellaneous services not formerly billed, and so forth.

If these pitfalls are to be avoided, several steps are required. First, physicians should be required to accept the allowable charge as full compensation for services. Second, fees should be established on a basis that will encourage a socially appropriate distribution of physicians by location and specialty, rather than on the basis of past patterns of physician charges. Third, adjustments in the fee schedule over time should be established in such a way as to constrain increases in total expenditures to an economic index, such as earnings in the economy.

The national health insurance bills that have been introduced in Congress share a commonality of goals. They try to (1) ensure that all persons have financial access to medical care, (2) eliminate the financial hardship of medical bills, and (3) limit the rise in health care costs.

Current Alternatives

In spite of this uniformity of goals, there is a wide variety of approaches from which to choose. The proposal backed by the American Medical Association relies on tax credits to induce greater coverage under private health insurance plans. Senators Russell B. Long and Abraham A. Ribicoff would replace Medicaid with a federal plan for the poor and cover catastrophic expenses for everyone. The administration, the American Hospital Association, and the Health Insurance Association of America have all backed bills that rely heavily on the purchase of basic and catastrophic private health insurance through employer groups, with government contributions for care of the poor and aged. The compromise plan advanced by Senator Edward M. Kennedy and Congressman Wilbur D. Mills relies more heavily on public insurance financed by payroll taxes and federal and state general revenues. The Health Security Act, originally introduced by Senator Kennedy and Congresswoman Martha W. Griffiths and still backed by the AFL-CIO, replaces private insurance with a federal program covering virtually all medical bills for U.S. residents.

These major bills, while quite different in approach, have some similarities. They would provide a wide range of benefits to nearly all of the population. Direct payments by patients are minimal or nonexistent for the lowest-income groups, and all covered persons, regardless of income, would be guaranteed some ceiling on contributions. Working families with annual incomes below about $8,000 to $10,000 would receive at least partial subsidies under most plans.

The major bills differ markedly, however, in the methods of financing, administration, and reimbursement of providers. Because some plans are financed primarily by private insurance premiums through employer groups, they retain a much larger share of expenditures in the private sector. Private health insurance companies stand to benefit considerably by such plans; employers would face much greater obligations for employee benefits; and the cost of the plans would ultimately fall much more heavily on lower-income working families. State governments, in most plans emphasizing private coverage, would have much greater responsibility for administering coverage for the poor and those not covered by employer groups and for regulating and controlling health insurance companies and medical care providers.

The principal similarities of the major national health insurance bills and the different impacts they may have are summarized below.

Population coverage.   All the plans would cover most of the population. The Health Security Act calls for universal coverage of all U.S. residents. The Long-Ribicoff bill would provide catastrophic benefits to persons of all ages who are insured or receiving benefits under social security, as well as basic benefits to all low-income people. Other bills would exclude small, but significant, fractions of the population. The Kennedy-Mills plan would not cover 3 million people—mostly young adults who are no longer eligible for their parents' plans and who have not yet had sufficient work experience to qualify for their own coverage. The administration plan would exclude 6.5 million people—mostly families with incomes above $5,000 who are not covered by employer groups, including the long-term unemployed, those newly or temporarily employed, part-time workers, families without an able-bodied worker, and the self-employed. The Health Insurance Association of America plan would not cover 25 million people— mostly those who do not currently have private health insurance, such as poor health risks, workers in small firms, workers in agricultural, construction, and retail trade industries, and the self-employed.

Range of medical benefits.   The most striking similarity among the major national health insurance bills before Congress is their emphasis on a comprehensive range of health services. All cover both inhospital and ambulatory services. All would cover skilled nursing-home care, with limits ranging from 30 days under the American Hospital Association plan to 180 days under the Health Insurance Association of America plan. The Kennedy-Mills plan would introduce a new program to provide long-term care for the elderly in a variety of settings. All except the American Medical Association and the Long-Ribicoff plans would cover prescription drugs. The administration and Kennedy-Mills plans emphasize family planning, maternity care, and well-child care. Dental services for children are provided under all plans except the Long-Ribicoff bill and the Health Insurance Association of America; the latter would provide one dental examination annually to adults and children.

Direct patient payments. (See Table 7-2 for a summary of patient liabilities under the various bills.) The Health Security Act would not require patients to contribute toward the cost of medical bills incurred; care would be provided free of charge for virtually all medical services. At the other extreme, the Long-Ribicoff plan would require families (except those with incomes below $4,800 for a family of four and $2,400 for a single individual) to pay for the first sixty days of hospital care, the first $2,000 of medical bills, and at most an additional $1,000 of coinsurance payments. Working families without private insurance to meet these payments would be subject to severe financial hardship in the event of a medical catastrophe.

Other plans incorporate moderate direct patient contributions for all except low-income families. The administration and Kennedy-Mills plans contain deductibles of $150 per person (for three family members in the administration bill and two family members in the Kennedy-Mills bill) and a coinsurance rate of 25 percent on bills exceeding the deductible. The trade association bills have more moderate patient cost-sharing requirements.

All plans reduce or eliminate cost sharing for low-income families and place a ceiling on family contributions. The maximum ceiling for the highest-income families is set at 10 percent of income under the American Hospital Association and American Medical Association plans, at $1,000 under the Kennedy-Mills and Health Insurance Association of America plans, and at $1,500 under the administration plan. Only the administration plan requires substantial patient payments for families with incomes below $5,000. Maximum ceilings are reduced for families with incomes below $8,000 to $10,000 in most plans.

While these ceilings should protect most families from severe financial hardships, a number of plans permit physicians to charge patients more than the amounts that would be paid by the insurance plan. These excess charges are not included in calculating maximum patient contributions, so that a patient undergoing complex surgery might receive a physician's bill several thousand dollars in excess of amounts that would be paid by the plans.

Costs of the plans. The cost study made in 1974 by the U.S. Department of Health, Education, and Welfare permits a comparison of the major national health insurance plans.[1] This study applies a uniform methodology to all plans to derive estimates of costs by sources of payment. One crucial assumption of this study is that the price controls proposed under Phase IV of the Economic Stabilization Program are in effect regardless of the provisions of a bill for controls on prices. Thus, the rate of price increase is assumed to be the same regardless of which, if any, bill is implemented.

Three concepts of costs are important: (1) real resource costs (total amount spent on medical care in the United States); (2) expenditures under the plan (excluding direct payments by patients and uncovered services); and (3) federal and state government expenditures. (See Tables 6-1 and 6-3 for a summary of cost estimates.) The net incremental impact on federal and state budgets is of course affected by funds that would be expended in any event and any changes in federal revenues that would occur.

The plans differ little in real costs, and those plans with higher costs simply reflect the greater use of medical services that they would generate. In terms of expenditures covered by the plan, the Long-Ribicoff plan would cover about 35 percent of all medical expenditures, while the Health Security Act would cover 82 percent. The total expenditure cost of the administration and Kennedy-Mills plans is about the same—$69 billion and $72 billion, respectively. The latter, however, would require $39 billion of added federal financing, while the administration plan, by relying on employer premiums as a major source of financing, would require only $6.3 billion of additional federal financing. State government expenditures (including local government outlays for charity hospital care) would be reduced in most plans.

Impact on employers. Any additional costs of national health insurance for employers are likely eventually to be borne either by consumers,

1. HEW, *Estimated Health Expenditures under Selected National Health Insurance Bills,* A Report to the Congress (1974).

in the form of higher prices, or by employees, in the form of lower wages than would have been earned without the insurance. However, any sudden marked change in the responsibilities of employers can have important short-run effects.

Employer contributions to health insurance coverage are estimated to increase from $20 billion in the absence of a national health insurance plan to $27 billion under the administration plan, and $35 billion in the American Hospital Association plan. Employers would be expected to contribute about $7 billion toward supplementary private insurance plans in the Kennedy-Mills bill; however, any employer facing a reduction in health insurance costs would be required to pay either the employee's share of the payroll tax or compensate employees for the reduction in his obligation.

The administration plan would require all employers to pay $390 per family in the first year. The American Hospital Association plan would set the employer contribution at $758 per family. These amounts greatly exceed current employer contributions, particularly in small firms and in service, finance, retail trade, and agricultural industries. The Health Insurance Association of America and American Medical Association plans would be voluntary for the employer and employee, and do not specify the employer's share of the premium (which would exceed $900 per family).

Limited federal subsidies to employers would be available for five years in the administration plan and for up to ten employees in the American Hospital Association plan. Even so, many firms that do not currently make significant contributions to health insurance plans would face substantial increases in labor costs.

Cost to individuals by income class. The cost of national health insurance, whether nominally paid by federal or state governments or by employers, must ultimately be borne by individuals. Of primary concern in the analysis of the cost of any national health insurance plan, therefore, is the distribution of that cost among persons of different income classes. (See Table 6-7 for the distribution of costs among income classes for the administration and Kennedy-Mills plans.)

When the costs of the two plans are compared with income, the administration plan is seen to be highly regressive over the entire income range. Families with incomes below $3,000 contribute 22 percent of their income to the plan, compared with 4 percent of income for families with incomes above $50,000. The cost of the Kennedy-Mills plan is distributed approximately in proportion to income, with the lowest-income and middle-income groups paying 7 to 8 percent of their income and the highest-income groups paying 5 percent.

While both the administration and the Kennedy-Mills plans receive some funds from federal and state general revenues, the principal difference in their sources of financing is the heavy reliance on premiums in the administration plan compared with a payroll tax on the first $20,000 of earnings in the Kennedy-Mills plan. This difference is reflected in the declining proportion of income devoted to national health insurance in the administration plan and the constant proportion of income (up to $20,000) applied to the Kennedy-Mills health insurance plan.

Effect on private insurance companies. The administration bill and the trade association plans would greatly increase sales and administered business (primarily administration of coverage for the poor and elderly) of private insurance companies. Combined sales and administered business would increase from about $55 billion without national health insurance to $80 billion under the administration plan and $90 billion under the American Hospital Association plan. The Health Insurance Association of America and American Medical Association plans would increase sales from $33 billion in 1975 without national health insurance to $62 billion, since under these plans even coverage for the poor would be through the subsidized sale of private health insurance.

The Kennedy-Mills plan and the Health Security Act would greatly reduce the role of private health insurance companies. While the Kennedy-Mills plan, like the administration plan, would result in $80 billion of sales and administered business, only $12 billion of that amount would represent sales, instead of $37 billion as in the administration plan. The Health Security Act would almost completely eliminate the private health insurance business.

Role of state governments. The Long-Ribicoff plan, the Kennedy-Mills bill, and the Health Security Act would all be federally run programs, with the federal government responsible for administration of the plan and establishing methods of paying medical care providers. State government participation would be limited to some contributions for care of the poor.

The administration and trade association plans would create a much larger role for state governments. They would be charged with the regulation and supervision of private health insurance companies and with the establishment of methods of reimbursing hospitals, physicians, and other providers of medical services. The American Medical Association plan, on the other hand, would reimburse all providers according to usual and customary charges, and no state or federal intervention would be permitted. The states would also be charged with the provision of insurance coverage to the poor (with federal subsidies and regulations) under the administration and Health Insurance Association of America plans.

Methods of payment for hospitals, physicians, and other providers. The methods of reimbursing providers of medical services range from unrestricted methods in the American Medical Association bill to fairly stringent curbs on payments under the Health Security Act. Most bills would favor moderate methods of reimbursement that attempt to leave physicians and hospitals with about the same average level of reimbursement as they currently earn. The administration and the Kennedy-Mills bills would try new methods of reimbursement, while the Long-Ribicoff bill would model reimbursement along the same lines as used in the Medicare program.

While precise methods of reimbursement are not spelled out, the administration and Kennedy-Mills plans would establish prospective methods of reimbursing hospitals and other institutions that would not depend on actual expenses incurred during the year. Physicians would be reimbursed according to a fee schedule that would probably vary by specialty and by geographical location. Any physician electing to do so could charge patients (other than poor and elderly patients in the administration plan) more than the established fee. Physicians electing to accept the established fee would receive some billing and collection advantages, but most physicians would probably opt for the more generous incomes they could derive by setting their own fees.

A Recommended Plan for National Health Insurance

While most of the national health plans contain several good features, none is without flaws. The administration and Kennedy-Mills plans are similar in benefit structure and should both be largely effective in meeting the major goals of national health insurance. The cost of the administration plan, however, falls heavily on lower-income working families, and the plan would be a boon to private health insurance companies and a bane to employers. The Kennedy-Mills plan, while distributing costs much more equitably among income classes, would require substantial increases in federal expenditures. Neither plan would effectively curb cost increases, and some segments of the population would be excluded from coverage under both plans.

Since evaluation of any given approach to national health insurance must carefully weigh the possible advantages and disadvantages, selection of a "best" plan is difficult. The following recommendations, however, outline the principal features of a national health insurance plan that would meet the major goals of ensuring access to care, avoiding financial hardships, and limiting the rise in medical care costs, while at the same time distributing the costs equitably among different income classes.

• *Universal coverage.* The plan should cover all U.S. residents and should not exclude anyone because of family composition, employment status, or social security contribution history.

• *Comprehensive benefits.* The plan should cover both inhospital and ambulatory services, including services of health centers or clinics, prescription drugs, preventive services for children, maternity and family planning services, dental services for children, and at least limited skilled nursing-home and mental health benefits. Services provided by paramedical personnel should be covered if provided under the supervision of a physician—whether the physician is physically present or not. The same broad, comprehensive benefits should be available to all families.

• *Direct patient payments.* Direct payments should not be required for low-income families (those, say, with incomes of less than $5,000 for a family of four). While moderate direct patient payments should be required for middle- and upper-income families (to reduce the cost of the plan and to encourage efficiency), some reduction in these amounts should be made for lower-income families (those, say, between $5,000 and $10,000). Ceilings should be placed on the maximum contributions to health care, required of any family.

One schedule meeting this general recommendation would include no cost sharing below $5,000, a deductible of $150 per person (for three family members), 25 percent coinsurance, and a ceiling of $1,000 for all families with incomes above $10,000. For families with incomes between $5,000 and $10,000, the ceiling could be set at 20 percent of income in excess of $5,000. These income classes and deductible and ceiling amounts should be automatically adjusted upward over time as income and medical expenditures increase.

If the Medicare program is retained for the elderly, comparable ceilings on patient payments should be added. The program for the elderly should gradually be modified over time to a structure similar to coverage for other persons.

• *Tax subsidies for supplementary insurance.* Purchase of supplementary insurance to pick up required direct patient payments should not be subsidized by tax provisions. Any contributions by employers to such plans should be counted as taxable income to the employee and a nonlegitimate business expense of employers. No personal income tax deductions for premiums of supplementary insurance should be permitted.

• *Financing.* The plan should be financed in such a way that the burden does not fall disproportionately on low-income families. A combination of general revenues and a tax on payroll and unearned income would be preferable—similar to the financing provided in the Kennedy-Mills plan. If financing instead relies on premiums by employers, a credit should be allowed for any premiums in excess of some percentage of payroll (such as 4 percent) to convert the impact of the premium from a fixed amount per worker to a fixed percentage of earnings.

• *Administration.* The plan should be administered by the federal government. Reimbursement of claims for segments of the population could be undertaken by private organizations or state governments on the basis of competitive bidding, with federal supervision, provided safeguards on the privacy of income information were installed. If private insurance companies are permitted to sell the standard insurance plan, premiums should not be permitted to exceed 10 percent of benefit expenses.

• *Consumers.* Consumers should be represented on all advisory boards. Grievance processes should be established for patients to file complaints about improper handling of claims or inadequacy of care provided.

• *Minorities and access to care.* Hospitals, physicians, and other providers should be prohibited from discriminating among patients on the basis of race, nationality, or creed. Procedures for enforcement of nondiscriminatory provisions should be incorporated in the plan, including site visits for compliance, administrative procedures for informing patients of rights, and processes of filing complaints of discriminatory treatment. A health resources development fund should be created and funds earmarked for programs that will increase the availability of medical resources in minority neighborhoods.

• *Rural residents and access to care.* Methods of reimbursement should encourage the creation and optimal utilization of medical resources in rural areas, including the establishment of fee schedules for physicians that reward rather than penalize physicians for practicing in underserved areas, and reimbursement for services rendered by paramedical personnel and rural health centers whether a physician is physically present when service is rendered or not. Funds of a health resources development board should be specifically targeted on personnel who desire to locate in rural communities and on the development of innovative approaches to health care delivery in rural areas. Supplementary programs to overcome specific barriers to medical care in rural areas—such as transportation services and coordination of medical and other services affecting health—should be developed.

• *Reimbursement of hospitals, physicians, and other providers.* Prospective methods of reimbursement for hospitals and other institutional providers should be developed and tried experimentally. Controls that place limits on per patient costs, similar to those in Phase IV of the Economic Stabilization Program, should also be considered. Limits should be placed on the incomes of such hospital-based specialists as anesthesiologists, radiologists, and pathologists.

Physicians and other noninstitutional providers should be required to accept the allowable charge as full compensation for services. Fees should be established on a basis that encourages a socially appropriate distribution of physicians by location and specialty rather than on the basis of past patterns of physician charges. Adjustments in the fee schedule over time should be established in such a way as to tie increases in total expenditures to an economic index, such as earnings in the economy.

Index

180   National Health Insurance

bursement under, 89, 163; state con-
tributions to, 142
Long, Russell B., 80, 166. *See also*
Long-Ribicoff bill
Luft, Harold, 68n

McAfee, Melbah, 47n, 156n
Major medical insurance, 37–38. *See
also* Catastrophic health insurance
Manheim, Larry M., 12n, 62n
Marshall, Ray, 47n
Medicaid, 1, 31; accomplishments of,
42–43; administrative expenses, 74,
75; benefits, 42, 44, 46–47; effect on
medical costs, 4; effect on physicians'
incomes, 13–14; emphasis on institutional care, 45; expenditures for, 41;
under HIAA plan, 103; percentage of
health insurance premiums to, 15–16;
replacement by AHA plan, 99; replacement by AHCIP, 91; replacement by Long-Ribicoff bill, 80, 85, 86,
87; restricted coverage by, 2, 3, 44; in
rural areas, 157, 158; shortcomings
of, 44; treatment of minorities under,
46–47, 155–57; variations in state
programs for, 45–46
Medical care: deficiencies in private
provisions for, 9–11; limited information on, 21–22; monopolistic conditions in market for, 22–23; public
versus private provisions for, 25–26
Medical Expense Tax Credit Act, 83–85
Medical technology, 5, 10, 25
Medicare, 1, 24, 31; administrative expenses, 72, 73; benefits, 50–51, 53–54;
catastrophic coverage under, 54–55;
effect on medical costs, 4; effect on
physicians' incomes, 13–14; federal
expenditures for, 50; FHCIP revision
of, 94–95; under HIAA plan, 103; in-
equity in benefits under, 51–53; under
medicredit proposal, 81, 83; premium
payments for, 50; regional differences
in benefits under, 53–54; reimbursement to physicians under, 77; replacement by AHA plan, 99; restricted
coverage by, 2, 54; in rural areas, 157,
158; shortcomings of, 50–51; supplementary medical insurance plan, 47,
50; treatment of minorities under, 53,
155–57
Medicredit proposal: benefits, 81–82,
168; cost of, 131, 133, 135, 139; coverage, 81–82; disadvantages of, 82–
83; effect on private insurance com-

panies, 171; employer contributions
to, 143, 145; reimbursement under,
131, 171–72; tax credits for, 135, 166
Mental health care, 58
Migrant workers, medical care for, 10,
54
Mills, Wilbur D., 80, 104, 166. *See also*
Kennedy-Mills bill
Minorities: coverage by private health
insurance, 37; hospital discrimination
against, 156–57; Medicaid benefits to,
46, 155–57; Medicare benefits to, 53,
155–57; physicians' discrimination
against, 156; under recommended national health insurance plan, 174
Mitchell, Bridger M., 15n, 16n
Monopoly in medical care market, 22–
23
Mosley, Peter, 26n
Mueller, Marjorie S., 17n, 73n

National health insurance: alternative
approaches to, 6–7; cost control aspects of, 4–5, 25, 162–65; employer
contributions to, 142–43, 145, 169–
70; federal expenditures for, 1, 7, 8,
31, 41, 50, 133; federal tax subsidies
for, 135, 137, 143, 145; goals of, 2–
6, 151–52, 161, 166; HEW cost study
of, 130–32; recommended plan for,
173–75; for rural areas, 157–59; state
expenditures for, 1, 7, 31, 41, 139,
142; treatment of minorities under,
155–57. *See also* Administration proposal for national health insurance;
American Hospital Association national health insurance plan; Financing national health insurance; Health
Insurance Association of America national health insurance plan; Health
Security Act; Kennedy-Mills bill;
Long-Ribicoff bill; Medical Expense
Tax Credit Act; Medicredit proposal
Newhouse, Joseph P., 13n, 23n, 62n, 63,
64, 67n, 77n, 130n
Nursing care, 19
Nursing homes: discriminatory practices against minorities by, 47, 157;
under Medicaid, 45, 47; under na-
tional health insurance, 59, 167–68

Okner, Benjamin A., 5n, 147n

Pauly, Mark V., 12n, 18
Payroll tax, 5, 29, 69–70, 72, 86
Pechman, Joseph A., 5n, 147n